KEEPERS

Radio Stories from Only A Game & Elsewhere

For my mother,
whose love and generosity have been constant;
For my mother-in-law,
a most loyal reader and listener;
For Amy and Alison,
who delight and surprise us every day;
But most of all,
for Mary.

KEEPERS

Radio Stories from Only A Game & Elsewhere

Bill Littlefield

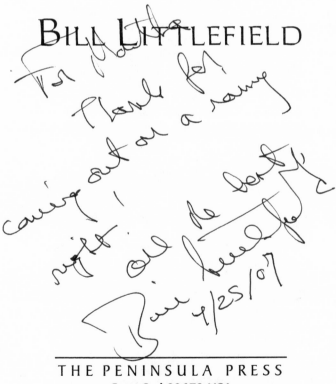

THE PENINSULA PRESS
Cape Cod 02670 USA

Published by
The Peninsula Press · Cape Cod 02670 USA
Donald W. Davidson
Publisher
The publisher is solely and fully responsible for the contents
of this edition, including any errors and omissions.

Front jacket image by
Jim Goodnough
Goodnough Photography
Brewster, MA 02631

Back jacket image by
Henry Horenstein
Boston, MA 02118

Cover reprographics by
Printastic, Inc.
South Yarmouth, MA 02664

Visit The Peninsula Press online:
www.capecod.net/peninsulapress
To e-mail The Peninsula Press: booksetc@capecod.net

Library of Congress Catalog Card Number: 97-80875
Littlefield, Bill
   KEEPERS: Radio Stories from Only A Game & Elsewhere
   The Peninsula Press, ©1998.
ISBN 1-883684-18-8

First edition
Manufactured in the United States of America
1 2 3 4 5 6 7 8 9 / 06 05 04 03 02 01 00 99 98

PREFACE

If ever I get to give a graduation speech, I'll say "I hope you all find work which you can enjoy as much as I enjoy mine."

I started writing commentaries for WBUR in 1984. NPR's *Morning Edition* began airing some of them shortly thereafter. For a chunk of time after that, my pieces ran on *Morning Edition* each Tuesday morning, while Frank Deford's ran on Monday and Red Barber talked with Bob Edwards on Friday. I'd be inclined to remember those as the best of times, except that in 1993 WBUR took a chance on *Only A Game*, which began as a half-hour local program with a staff of three people: David Greene, Gary Waleik, and myself. We had two desks and three chairs in an office so small that one of us had to be out on a story at all times. Good plan by somebody.

Almost all of the pieces in this collection aired on WBUR, *Morning Edition*, or *Only A Game*. I hope you enjoy them, whether again or for the first time.

BILL LITTLEFIELD
Boston, 1998

INTRODUCTION

The tenth anniversary of *Morning Edition* seemed an appropriate time to give some thought to the place of sports on public radio.

For the sake of argument, why do our games have *any* place in a news program at all? There's enough serious matter to fill two hours each day. The rain is poison; we can't afford health care; and the homeless are legion in our streets. How can we take time — even only a little time — for baseball and basketball, let alone (God help us!) football and golf?

Well, whatever large numbers of us choose to care about is "news." And large numbers of people care passionately about sports. That's one argument.

Then there is the case for art. Michael Jordan at work — or better, Michael Jordan erasing for a moment the distinction between work and play while we watch — has a claim on genius. Emily Dickinson once said she knew a *real* poem, because when she read it, it would blow the top of her head off. Basketball fans might say the same in the presence of Jordan's acrobatics, which are as hard-earned and far beyond the rest of us as the skills of a great poet or musician. Art, in whatever form, lifts our spirit and gives us, temporarily, something splendid to dream on, and some sense of human potential that we might otherwise lose sight of in our efforts to make sense of each day. Call that escape, if you like, but if you do, listening to Chopin or Charlie Parker, and viewing a Monet and reading William Faulkner are also escapes.

Paying attention to sports provides us with matter as valid as any for finding out what it's like to be alive in the world. We see skill and luck in every game, of course, and maybe we learn something about how they balance. In the accelerated process of aging that even the most spectacularly successful athletes must confront, we get a kind of practice run for our own decline. In the closing of some careers we see dignity, even grace. In many more we see what Dylan Thomas called "raging against the dying of the light," and we can try to decide (if we choose to be judgmental about it) whether that or dignity is preferable.

Another attraction here — though not one likely to convince skeptics of the newsworthiness of sports — is that we can understand what we are seeing or listening to. In school, I had a friend who used to ask people questions he knew they could answer. In the presence of so many they couldn't answer, he knew it would make them feel better. He'd ask them things like "What time is it?" or "When's lunch?" Sports, happening within clear, white lines and providing final scores offers us similar comfort. Whatever doubts we may have about the president's motivation or his competence; however precarious the balance of the Supreme Court, when we hear that the A's have beaten the Giants in 4 straight, we *know* something.

If all this is unnecessary for you — if you're satisfied with the niche that the discussion of sports occupies in your news program — then sorry for the misuse of time when I might have been talking about trades, goals, aces, or touchdowns.

Indulge me here.

However long I'm at it, there's still apparently the recurrent need to convince myself.

SPRING

OF HEROES & HEROINES

A couple of years ago, *Only A Game* ran a contest inviting listeners to tell us what athlete they most would like to be or to have been and why.

Many of the contest entries mentioned Jesse Owens. That was impressive. But the whole experience of this competition turned out to be great fun for a lot of reasons. There was, for example, the surprise of discovering the variety of athletes people chose to be: Willie Mays and Martina Navratilova; Babe Didrickson and Pele; Sonja Henie and Pee Wee Reese; Mary Lou Retton and Bill Bradley; Joan Benoit Samuelson and Arnold Palmer and Bill Buckner and Jackie Robinson and Charlie Brown and Mickey Mouse and so on and on.

Many of the entries were not only creative and funny, but genuinely life-affirming. Alison Mack of Wilmington, Delaware, wrote: "I'd be Victor, a tow-headed boy I still remember from 5th grade. He long-jumped further than anyone, only to fall over backwards, grin, and try again. Victor came in last that day back in 1970, but I bet he's since lived up to his name."

Who'd have thought that our contest would have encouraged somebody to remember a failed long jump 25 years gone? Victor, I hope you read this. You've got a fan.

Kevin Rorabaugh of Ellis, Kansas, worked a childhood

theme into his entry, too, but his pick had a practical slant. He said he'd like to be the batboy for the 1970 World Champion Baltimore Orioles, not only because he'd have been able to hang around his heroes, but because the Orioles voted their batboy a full series share that season: $18,216.

Peaco Todd of Somerville, Massachusetts, struck a note at once mournful and stoic with this tribute: "I would be Satchel Paige: knowing that while I am the best there is, or maybe ever will be, I will play the length of my career dim in the shadow of the majors, and keep my heart intact while I wait for history to shine its light on me."

Charlie Combs e-mailed from the Berklee School of Music in Boston: "Since I'm in theater, I'd like to be Joe DiMaggio so that Marilyn Monroe could introduce me to Arthur Miller . . . Now, there's a guy who could make the *plays.*"

That entry might have won if we had put a greater emphasis upon quirkiness, but it would have had competition from Jack Cahill, who wrote: "In August, 1978, Bill Lee out-pitched Jim Palmer 1-0 at Fenway Park. The rowdy crowd quickly quieted" (that's some phrase, Mr. Cahill) "the rowdy crowd quickly quieted to focus on the nine-inning duel: Baltimore's masterful right-hander versus the truest lefty God *ever* made. There, in the full knowledge and exult of Lee's moment, is where I want to be."

Respondents did not limit themselves to choosing human athletes. Several would like to have been Secretariat. Sandi Goldberg of Somerville, Massachusetts, went for Man o' War, of whom she wrote: "Although I believe he was aware of his status as a champion, he ran for the sheer joy of tasting the wind in his mouth . . . and *what* a middle age he had!"

Some folks evidently had to sweat to make the 50-word limit, and some simply ignored it. But Jesse Gunther of Milo, Maine, made it work for him. His single-sentence entry read: "I would be Lou Gehrig at Yankee Stadium on July 4th, 1939, because he was telling the truth."

Family was a theme in a lot of responses. From Shoreline,

Washington, Bill Brown's was: "Let me fly past defenders with a wink. For a day, a season, give me the grace of Calvin Hill. Give me a son as blessed as Grant."

Another family-oriented entry from a listener who probably isn't actually old enough to have entered the contest ran like this: "If I could be any athlete in time, I would be my sister. Her room is filled with trophies for baseball, track, and gymnastics. Every sport she tries she does well in. I don't. I can't even swim well. And she is smart, too. She's talking about going to medical school."

From a slightly different perspective, Viera Wallace-Lorencova wrote that she'd like to be her own daughter 25 years hence as she becomes the first woman to win the Boston Marathon outright.

And looking back, rather than forward, Martin Gibson of Glen Cove, Maine, wrote a poem that begins:

I sit beside my father's bed,
*   this 5-foot 7 set shot-era guard.*
Rodman pays more in fines
*   than he made in a lifetime.*
I rode the bench, still he came . . .

And that ends:

I throw up a prayer
*   for fatherless children everywhere.*

Thanks to all who entered, I feel better about sports and about what they mean to people than I have felt in some time. And better about writing, too, which turns out not to be such a lost art after all.

ᕒ

I Wish I were a Pitcher

Oh, I wish I were a pitcher . . .
    I wish that I could throw
'em 90 miles an hour . . .
    But even were I slow,
I'd have a job in these times
    of pitchers in demand.
They'll sign you if you have a pulse.
    They'll pay you just to stand
out on the mound and look as if
    you might get someone out;
And if you *do*, your agent will
    emerge with so much clout . . .
And fourteen teams will bid for you
    when they hear what you've done.
They'll offer you the moon and stars.
    They'll offer you the sun.
They'll heap vast treasures at your feet
    as they hand you the pen.
(This is whether or not you ever or *never*
    get anyone out again.)

Boy, I wish I were a pitcher . . .
    I'd know just how to play it.
    Whatever the ballclub asked me to say,
    I go out there and say it.

13

I'd wrap my shoulder up in ice,
    I'd never punch a door,
or drink in bars where there were fights,
    or denigrate the poor,
dumb, working slobs who pay the freight
    and come to watch me pitch.
I'd say they were the *greatest* fans,
    and I would never switch
that judgment while I worked there.
    I'd never let them down.
I'd swear that they were number one
    'til I was out of town.

God, I wish I were a pitcher,
    and after the game was done,
out back in the players' parking lot
    (whether I had lost or won)
the girls would swarm my car and me
    and shout and scream my name,
and beg me to let them in with me,
    but I'd tell 'em all the same:
"Can't help you, ma'am. I love my wife.
    I gotta go home and be true,
'cause Wheaties makes it worth my while
    and pays me as long as I do.
And keeps my face on the cereal box,
    which all the managers see,
so the next time they need a pitcher,
    they'll probably call up me."

Gee, I wish I were a pitcher,
    Even though it's not all cake.
I know that pitchers get hurt sometimes,
    and the pressure, for goodness sake,
is brutal if you're in a pennant drive,
    and you give up the big home run,
but even then, I bet it would be
    plenty of good, clean fun,
because win or lose, and play or sit,
    and injured or strong as a moose,

they have to keep on paying you,
    unless they turn you loose.
And if they do that, you needn't fret,
    just let your agent know.
He'll find a team that wants you still,
    more than you could ever know.
And you'll sign your name,
    and they'll give you the bank.
They'll inform the press, and then
    you'll take your act on down the road
and do it all over again.

WHAT PRICE GLORY?

A couple of weeks ago, I was helping a friend of mine move, when I met a guy — a friend of the friend — who was wearing a high school letter jacket. And it wasn't just *any* high school letter jacket. It was red, not much faded, and he'd taken care of it. It had leather sleeves, white. And on the chest there was a superbly gaudy winged foot, silver and red, with a lot of little gold-colored medals pinned to it. This guy had been a track man.

But he'd been a track man 23 years ago. Because across the back of the jacket were the words: "Something Champs — 1966" . . . something, I don't know "State," "Division," I can't remember, but I remember the 1966.

This guy was a good mover, by the way. He handled his end of the sleeper sofa as well as any of us. I liked him. But I never quite worked up the nerve to ask him why he was still wearing his high school letter jacket.

One year when I was a little boy, the U.S. Open Golf Tournament was held at a country club close to where I lived. The man who lived next door to us was a member of that club, and he got to be a marshall for the tournament. That was not such a big deal, as I understood it. It probably meant that he was responsible for standing by a rope that stretched down the fairway to prevent the spectators from surging onto the course or otherwise bothering the golfers. But it also entitled him to a parking sticker which got him a preferred spot each day at the club during the Open. And the point of all this is that the sticker stayed on the guy's car for years after the tournament was over.

I asked my father about that one time — why our neighbor still had his sticker for the Open on the car — and my father said, "Because he's a jerk," which may have been true, but I think it was probably more complicated than that.

Last weekend I told these two stories to a neighbor of mine — a guy who is decidedly not a jerk, a 50-some-year-old ex-athlete who still plays tennis every weekend. We were walking around the block — he and his wife, my wife and I — and when I'd finished the stories there was this odd pause, as if nobody knew what to say, and then my friend's wife started to giggle.

"If you come over when we get back to the house," she said. "I'll show you his high school letter sweater. It's right in the hall closet."

In a class I teach called Writing About Sports, I used to give the students an exercise to do involving matters of this sort. I'd say, "Imagine you're walking down the street and coming the other way there's this guy who looks like he's 40 or so, and he's wearing his high school letter jacket. What do you make of him?" I always assumed they'd write pieces about how sad it was, how pathetic, that anyone would still be carrying around glory that old on his back, and usually that's exactly what they did write about.

But we might have been wrong, they and I. That guy I conjured up for the class may have been much more representative than I had thought, as well as representative of something other than what I had assumed.

Perhaps there are thousands — even *millions* — of high school state champ jackets and letter sweaters in the closets of the middle-aged among us . . . and maybe more people than we think take them out and wear them; if not in public, then in the privacy of their own homes. And for them the spring's most poignant sports stories have nothing to do with which of the Final Four will win, or how far the Oilers can go without Gretzky. They are watching Tommy John at the age of 45 trying to pitch for the Yankees and Steve Carlton, at 44, trying to pitch for anyone.

And they are wondering how — no matter *how* bad the debts, *how* dire the times — *how* could Pete Rose have sold the bat he used to get more hits than anyone?

ρ

Upon a Reading of Our Rites

The sports section of the Sunday *New York Times* included an astonishingly irresponsible column about spring training. Writing from Boca Raton a week before he really had to be there, George Vecsey groused about the metal barricades that separate the players from the fans at some facilities. He complained that spring training had gone the way of the family farm, which has been lost to faceless, corporate agribusiness. He moaned about northern ticket scalpers, and he yearned for the days when children might talk with their favorite players or even play a little catch with them. He claimed that any kid who tried that these days would be arrested or gassed.

Now, I'm not suggesting that Mr. Vecsey is wrong. I've visted eight or ten spring training camps over the years, and I've seen some unlyrical things. But you don't write that Santa Claus ought to cut down on the Christmas cookies and watch his cholesterol. You don't warn kids away from the Easter Bunny because the furry little guy might be rabid. And no sportswriter with any sense of what spring training means to the nation should be peppering his early baseball pieces with terms like "barricade," "ticket scalper," and "stun gun."

Each year, spring training signals the end of winter stories about the infielder who's angry about having to honor his contract and play for a million and a half a year when he thinks he ought to be getting two, the pitcher who's been arrested for trying to buy cocaine, and the first baseman's palimony suit. Spring training is about players renewing acquaintances, tossing balls to one another like boys, stretching in the warm sun like cats. After months of scraping the ice off your windshield and ruinous heating bills, spring training is about new green grass *somewhere*. It is about the promise of the return of the game. For the huge majority of baseball fans who will never actually see a day of spring training anywhere, it is an illusion as necessary as fair play.

So for shame, George Vecsey, and get a hold of yourself. Remember what you're there for. Grant us these days of sunshine and dreaming, of soft games of flip, and of smiling players signing baseballs and baseball cards for free until the last child has wandered away satisfied.

Give us our spring training.

And if you cannot find somewhere in yourself the requisite charity for that, call home for a replacement and go write about football.

⚑

Women Behind Home

It was just a squib in the paper the other day . . . a few lines of filler at the bottom of the page in the middle of my sports section, so you might have missed it.

San Francisco Giant manager Roger Craig said he was against having women umpires in the major leagues. He said it wasn't that he thought Pam Postema, who has been umpiring at the Triple A level for some years now, was a bad umpire; it was rather that, well, in Craig's own words, "the abuse you have to take as an umpire is terrible, and I just don't think women should have to take that kind of abuse."

Craig's comment wasn't nearly as bizarre as the one that Houston pitcher Bob Knepper let fly last spring, when he cited Biblical evidence that women shouldn't be umpires. But Roger Craig is no crank. He is a baseball man, a fellow who has spent his life in the game . . . and perhaps that's the problem.

Maybe he's never been around the house enough to see women put up with the abuse that a two year old can deliver on a really cranked-up day . . . abuse that makes a dirt-kicking, belly-bumping Billy Martin or Pete Rose look like an amateur. Maybe he hasn't read beyond the sports pages of the newspaper, so he hasn't encountered any of the studies which people are always doing that indicate that —

despite the growing number of women who are working now — females are still underpaid in comparison to men doing the same or similar work.

Maybe he doesn't watch anything but ballgames on TV. If so, the commercials he sees are mostly for beer, and the people who sell it are mostly men. But elsewhere on the dial the advertising industry is still presenting women as water-heads who swoon with delight over the prospect of a new, improved kitchen floor wax and who dance around the toilet bowl before cleaning it. Now *there's* some abuse worth worrying about.

Leaving aside the question of whether *anybody* should have to put up with the kind of abuse which major league managers sometimes give to umpires, maybe it's worthwhile to speculate on how well women would handle the shouting, the profanity, and the posturing.

According to statistics, plenty of them would be familiar with it, having endured similar behavior from fathers or husbands in situations where there weren't any rules written down. It seems to me that the folks looking to fill vacancies in the umpiring ranks ought to recognize that experience counts.

Of course, there will be people who'll try to take avantage of the change when it comes. Somewhere out there awaits a manager who'll field a line-up of Adonis look-alikes when the first woman umpire finally is hired, figuring that any woman is putty in the hands of a handsome young guy. It is, apparently, the same theory that George Bush has embraced in picking a running mate.

Come to think of it, maybe by the time Pam Postema or some other woman jumps to the bigs, no manager will be dumb enough to try it.

OPENING DAY, 1985

"I remember Ty Cobb," the old man said,
    And he did, you could tell by his eyes.
  "I saw his last year with the '28 A's
    And he hit almost .325.

He was still playing hard, though, at age 42,
    He was no longer quick as a cat.
  But this stuff about Rose and the record he's chasing . . .
    Pete Rose couldn't carry Cobb's bat."

His son sipped his coffee and nodded a little.
    He knew well enough to agree.
  "You remember the first game you took me to, Dad?
    Polo Grounds . . . '52? '53?

To get to the box seats we walked through a tunnel.
    It was crowded and musty and dark.
  Then suddenly there was the green of the outfield
    In that funny-shaped, screwy old park."

"Well, damn!" roared the old man. "I buy you a box seat,
    And take off the day from the store,
And all you remember is how green the grass was
    Where they don't even play any more?"

They laughed, and between them a boy kicked the table
    And pushed at the food on his plate.

23

If his dad and his grandpa kept talking and laughing,
    He knew they were gonna be late.

So he snatched up his glove and he punched at the pocket,
    As if that might move them along,
    But his father and grand dad weren't paying attention,
    Lost in an old baseball song.

"Babe Ruth," said the old man, "and Frankie Crosetti,
    DiMag, and the great Jimmy Foxx."
    "Gil Hodges, Pete Reiser, Duke Snider," his son cried,
    "And those soft hands at third . . . Billy Cox."

The old man was murmuring "Leo Durocher,
    Pie Traynor, Waite Hoyt, Dazzy Vance."
    "Ernie Banks," said his son. "Willie Mays, Bobby Thompson."
    The little boy just looked askance.

Who were all these guys that his father remembered?
    Who danced in his grandfather's eyes?
    And then, in a moment, the little boy saw it,
    And much to his father's surprise,

He said, "Mike Schmidt, Dave Stieb, and Aurelio Lopez,
    Fred Lynn, Jimmy Rice, and Tom Seaver,
    Wade Boggs, Reggie Jackson, and Willie Hernandez,
    Who's maybe the game's best reliever.

Steve Carlton, Dwight Gooden, Kent Hrbek, Don Sutton,
    Steve Garvey, Bill Caudill, George Brett,
    Tony Gwynn, Sweet Lou Whitaker, Pedro Guerrero,
    Rusty Staub, who still hits for the Mets."

The old man looked at his son; the son looked at his boy;
    There wasn't a lot left to say.
    Together they got up and went to the ballpark,
    Because it was Opening Day.

THE TRIUMPHANT COMBINATION

Earlier this spring, sports got its best old man story in some time when Jack Nicklaus charged down the last few holes at Augusta to win the 50th edition of the Masters Golf Tournament. You've heard from any number of celebrants about how that dramatic victory held off time and change.

Then on Tuesday night we got the best young kid story in quite a while when Roger Clemens struck out 20 Seattle Mariners and became the all-time major league leader in that particular specialty.

Jack Nicklaus is 46, and even if he hadn't won the Masters a sixth time, his place high among the most successful golfers ever would have been secure. Roger Clemens is not quite 24. He has yet to win his 21st game in the major leagues. But even if he were to decide today that he really wanted to be a fireman or the engineer on a locomotive rather than a pitcher for the Red Sox, his fame would be assured. His hat and his shoes and his beaming face are in the Baseball Hall of Fame now with those of Cy Young, Walter Johnson, and Satchell Paige. And none of those guys ever struck out 20 men in a major league game.

Jack Nicklaus is not only a superb golfer, he is a consummate television performer, as comfortable in front of the TV camera as he is standing over a two-foot, $50,000 putt.

25

His victory delighted every sports fan who values handsome grace under pressure and competitive fire banked with years of experience.

The triumph of Roger Clemens the other night was altogether different. When injuries benched him last year, Clemens was baffled. He wondered superfluously around the ballpark, his treacherous arm hanging worthless as a sausage. At 23, he began to hear people talk about his career in the past tense. When interviewed, he usually looked a little goofy: moon-faced, innocent, victimized. Last winter he had an operation on his shoulder, and he didn't even learn to snap at writers who asked how his arm felt until the end of spring training.

Clemens has little in common with Nicklaus, save that neither may ever do anything so publicly dramatic again. But that hardly matters. Within weeks of each other, the old master and the overpowering boy — each in the context of his own game — have reminded us of one reason why we play and watch and talk about sports so much. The golfer and the pitcher have reminded us that in the fleeting context of a golf match or a baseball game, at least, an individual can still hope to combine will and strength and luck to be unassailingly triumphant.

ₚ

TAKING TIME

It will be news to nobody that A. Bartlett Giamatti, the former commissioner of baseball, valued nearly everything that has to do with the game: the geometry of its yards, the skill of its players, the wonderful talk of its old men. *Take Time For Paradise* extols these pleasures delightfully. Subtitled *Americans and their Games*, this book is the published celebration of his game in all its glory.

But this book does a great deal more than remind us of what fun our best game can be to play and watch and remember. Ever the scholar as well as the fan, Giamatti makes a compelling case for baseball as evidence that — although we are imperfect as a species — we can nonetheless strive for perfection (what he calls "freedom of the spirit.")

Our invention of baseball to fill our leisure time, along with the decision we've made to follow it closely and to care about it passionately, all seem to Mr. Giamatti evidence that we yearn to be better than we are: more ordered, more graceful, more nearly harmonious with the world in which we find ourselves. It's an intriguing mix of renaissance scholarship with an appetite for baseball, which yields some curious couplings.

"There are no dragons in baseball, only shortstops, but they can emerge from nowhere to cut one down," says

Giamatti late in the book. This learned fellow who knew intimately the work of dragons *and* shortstops earned the right to discuss the game in a context that some will find precious and that some lost souls may even mock. But if your imagination is alive, you'll love this book.

"It is not news that there is the snake of error in our lives," he writes. "The news occurs when, for a moment, we can kill it."

When have you heard anyone express more perfectly the magic attraction of this hard game?

Even if you're dubious, entertain for a moment the possibility that Giamatti is right when he says "the gods are brought back when people gather" and implies that an old ballpark with a grass field as green as the garden we've lost is as perfect a place for gathering as we're ever likely to find.

Giamatti was, of course, aware of baseball as a large and lucrative business. He knew well enough that owners could be clods; that players could be spiteful, arrogant and childish; that agents could be crooks. Read this book and you'll see why he never let such knowledge get him down.

What sustained him was the good-natured conviction that baseball is more than the sum of its sometimes disappointing parts and that in its best moments the game is a window to some ideal we can otherwise find only in art. Who else would so convincingly compare the energy in a sonnet to the energy in a double play?

Take Time For Paradise is brief, as wit usually is. It is full of love and wonder and reverence. It displays Giamatti's considerable range of enthusiasms and his mastery of various contexts. Toward the end of the book he recounts with glee the conversations he overheard or joined in the lobby of the Marriot Pavillion Hotel during the National League Championship Series in 1987. He gives as the various fans, from the religiously obsessed to the goofy and drunk; and the baseball men, of course: the scouts, the farm directors, the minor league general managers and others; and there are the groupies, the sharpies, the hangers-on; the deal-makers, the ticket hustlers. Well, you get the point. Bart Giamatti in his love for the sport in all of its possibilities was as comfortable among all these as he was among the dragons in the garden; as delighted by them as he was by the bright ring of a new image for a true idea.

Take Time For Paradise, published posthumously, will make his readers miss him all over again.

OPENING DAY, 1987

Remember 1927?
    Let me help you out.
    The Yankees had a club that year . . .
        Some say without a doubt
    the greatest that there ever was
        and maybe it's the truth.
    They had Meusel, Coombs, and Gehrig,
        and, of course, they had Babe Ruth.
    With sixty homers Babe was one
        of baseball's brightest suns —
    In the shade behind him, Gehrig knocked in
        near two hundred runs.

They won one hundred ten games . . .
    only played one fifty four.
    That was sixty years ago now . . .
        And twenty years before
    the baseball world would finally crack
        six decades of disgrace
    by making room for Robinson,
        who made himself a place
    on Brooklyn's long-loved Dodgers,
        who were also called "the bums"
    and who drew their fans from everywhere
        with horns and bells and drums.

They filled the seats at Ebbets Field
   (we thought they always should),
and in a world of justice, Lord,
   I s'pose that they still would.
But in 1957,
   merely thirty years ago,
O'Malley moved the ball club west
   and as they watched it go,
the tears slid down the faces
   of the fans without a team,
as they cursed the lure of money,
   and they wept to lose a dream.

And in L.A. the Dodgers never
   see themselves as bums,
but as the pals of movie stars,
   who come to eat the crumbs
off Tom Lasorda's table
   when he leaves them any there,
which can't be very often,
   by the way he fills a chair . . .

But I digress, I stray,
   I wander, dawdle, balk, and roam.
I only meant to say that since
   the Brooklyn Bums left home
it's thirty years . . . and forty since
   Jack Robinson first thrilled
the Bums' fans with his courage
   and the Jim Crow that he killed.
And sixty years — gee, sixty —
   since the '27 Yanks
rolled through the league like soldiers
   in a row of armored tanks.

In the ballparks only hours from now
   another season starts . . .
of hitters who can lash line drives
   and pitchers throwing darts,
of boys who're cracking line-ups
   and of old men hanging on,

31

Of summer afternoons that
   seem to linger for so long
that sixty years, or thirty years,
   is just a moment gone.
And one day, twenty years from now,
   or thirty, or three score,
what happens on the field today
   will multiply the lore
that calls up Ruth and Gehrig,
   Jackie Robinson, and more,
the sunlit grass of Ebbets Field,
   gone summer's boys at play.
We start another chapter now . . .
   Good Morning, Opening Day.

Who are You?
And What's that Game You're Playing?

I don't know a lot about soccer (a condition that will become more and more apparent as this story lopes along), but I don't know a lot about darts, either, or chess, or the luge, and I've written about all of *them*. I figured I'd make up for the absence of expertise with enthusiasm and the willingness to be where the story was, even before it was there. That's why I was standing on the edge of the field at Foxboro Stadium when the U.S. team finished its final practice just before beating the English team, and Great Britain collapsed into self-loathing.

But one thing at a time. I, of course, recognized nobody among the players coming off the practice field. I picked one at random and asked him a few questions. In a faint Scottish accent he expressed confidence in his team and faith that soccer would catch on in this country. These were not revolutionary sentiments, but they were serviceable. When we'd finished talking, I asked the young man his name. For a beat and a half he looked at me incredulously. Then he said, "John Harkes."

I learned later that Harkes is one of the few U.S.-born players who has reached the top rank of competition overseas. He's a star for the delightfully named Sheffield Wednesday Club in the English League, and he was the first U.S. player to compete in England's Football Association Cup Final. My asking him his name was roughly equivalent to an English interviewer making the same inquiry of Michael Jordan . . . or, at least, John Harkes looked at me as if he felt that way.

My theory is that that's why Harkes and his teammates beat the English team the next evening. They were mad at me. Anyway, the unexpected 2-0 win was a very large deal in England. The more rational tabloids called for the coach's resignation. The others wanted him executed. I know this, because the day after the game I got my first phone call ever from the BBC. A man in Bristol wanted to know if the Americans were dancing in the streets. I looked out the window. "Not right now," I said.

"Well," he said, "we have the headlines from the Boston paper. It says, *Blimey! U.S. Boots the Brits!* It says, *All's Not Jolly For England!*"

"Right," I said. "But the headline that says, *Look Out Below — Red Sox Fall Under .500!* is bigger."

The man in Bristol was undeterred. "Still," he said, "it must have been something. Was everyone packed into the pubs watching the game on the telly?"

"A lot of people were watching the National Hockey League Finals," I said. "And the NBA Championship's final round. The soccer game wasn't on."

"What about hooligans?" the man from Bristol asked.

"I don't know what they were watching," I said.

That may have been where he gave up on the interview, because there was a pause, like the one that came after I asked John Harkes his name. Probably there was a producer giving the man in Bristol the "cut" sign through the window of a booth. Or maybe he was holding up one finger to signify that the man in Bristol should lob the yank one more question, then bail out.

"Well, what about you?" the man in Bristol asked, and he didn't have to actually say, *you nit!* "What's this game going to mean to you?"

"I'll try to keep an open mind," I said, trying to be

helpful. "I'll go to the video store and rent *One Hundred Greatest Soccer Goals*. I mean *Football* . . . *Football Goals*, right?"

There was no answer, so I repeated, "football . . . football, right?" a couple more times before I realized the line was dead.

ʅ

THE SPELL OF THE GOLF

I think I have finally discovered the perfect television sport, and it is golf.

Last weekend I was watching a baseball game on television — a pretty tense ball game that could have gone either way in the ninth inning. And when it was over, I didn't get out of the couch fast enough to switch off the set before the golf came on. That's what people who watch the sport on TV call it: *the golf.* It's a generic term, and except in rare cases, such as the Masters Tournament that Jack Nicklaus recently won, which specific event you're watching doesn't matter at all.

So, *the golf.*

It began to wash over me in shades of green, and it was striking. Here came all these impossibly clean-cut guys, spiffy beyond words, striding purposefully along miles and miles of manicured lawn. Not a slob or sorehead among them. Nobody spitting tobacco, nobody beet-red and raging at a referee. One after another these slender, nordic-looking lads and a tiny sprinkling of minorities identically whacked their golf balls through the clear, blue sky and solemnly (without surprise) watched them come to rest on the clipped grass hundreds of yards away just where they wanted them to be, while cultured-sounding commentators murmured their approval.

My appreciation for this show should not be confused with actually playing golf. Whatever inclination there might have been in that direction disappeared when I was about eight. My father cut down a 5 iron, gave me a lesson, and we repaired to the links. It was hot and muggy, and the grass was burned-out and prickly. I hooked my first shot through the windshield of a maintenance department jeep. Stupid game.

But golf on television . . . it feels like something Walt Disney might have thought up with Barry Manilow's help. Even a really bad shot lands in pristine sand or a sparkling pond.

Maybe it's the indisputable cleanness of the sport that makes it so attractive to a television audience which gleeful advertisers have learned is well-heeled and prone to buy the best, whether cars, clothes, or lawn care equipment. For whatever reason, the public's attitude toward golf on television definitely differs from its attitude toward other sports programming.

Watch baseball on TV this weekend and somebody is likely to shout, "Have you got that damn game on again?"

Watch golf and that same person will tread softly and speak in a whisper, if at all . . . under the spell of *the golf.*

BROUGHT TO YOU BY . . .

Louis Sullivan, Secretary of Health and Human Services, wants consciousness-raising *now,* and I'm for that.

At least some of the links between the tobacco companies and organized sports are as foul, dishonest, and vile as he has suggested. The development and promotion of Virginia Slims — a cigarette which has helped American women achieve a rate of lung cancer equal to that of their fathers, husbands, and sons — is gruesome enough. The coupling of the product with the athletic efforts of some of the world's best tennis players is, as Secretary Sullivan suggests, "immoral," or at least sneaky and unprincipled.

The juxtaposition of topflight women's tennis, which requires excellent conditioning, with a product which robs the people who use it of their health would be funny if the consequences of smoking weren't so sad. At least in the context of tennis, Secretary Sullivan's suggestion that sports fans should consider boycotting events sponsored by tobacco companies is compelling. Moral suasion and public flogging haven't accomplished anything. A blow to the wallet is a good idea.

But the association between the tobacco companies and some of the other sports they sponsor is murkier territory. Consider, for example, the Camel GT automobile races or the

Winston 500. Perhaps we have the coupling of more compatible partners here. While it is inconceivable that somebody on a respirator or a heart-lung machine could compete against Gabriella Sabatini, you don't have to breathe especially well to jam your foot to the floor of a car. I know from the letters inspired by last year's screed against the Indy 500 that auto racing fans don't go to the track to see death. But it's certainly undeniable that "the fellow in the bright nightgown" (as W.C. Fields called the reaper) casts a shadow over the place.

People rarely die playing tennis, but driving cars fast in heavy traffic has knocked off lots of folks. So has smoking cigarettes. People don't drive competitively in order to die, of course. People don't smoke cigarettes to commit suicide, either, but an awful lot of inadvertent death and debilitating injury have been associated with each activity. Maybe that pairing isn't as inherently ludicrous as the association between tobacco and tennis. Maybe Winston cigarettes and the Winston 500 deserve each other.

Secretary Sullivan, the occupant of an important and (I hope) an influential office, can't indulge in distinctions this frivolous. He is trying to publicize the shameless merchandising of death by means of an activity to which a large segment of the American public is addicted: watching sports.

For the health of all those involved, I hope he succeeds.

I hope the Women's Tennis Tournaments will one day be sponsored by a fiber-filled bread or a yogurt with no cholesterol.

And, darn it, I don't have so much against the auto racing fans that I want them to breathe poison, either.

Still, I don't know how the Bran Muffin GT Races or the Sugarless Bubblegum 500 would draw.

OPENING DAY, 1988

Suppose that you got up this morning —
    Oh, an hour or so ago —
   And suppose that you lived close enough to the ballpark . . .
    Suppose you decided to go.
  And you had in your closet an old flannel shirt,
    Like the Browns and the Senators wore,
 And you carried your baseball shoes out to the front steps,
    So they wouldn't scratch up the wood floor;
 And you left your long shirttail outside of your pants,
    Because who's gonna see you to care?
 And you walked to the ballpark (you lived *that* close),
    And in no time, it seemed, you were there.

And suppose now that someone (a groundskeeper, say)
    Left the clubhouse door open a crack.
  So you walk right on in there as if you belong
    Past the lockers and the empty bat rack
 And out through the tunnel that leads to the dugout . . .
    And your spikes on the concrete . . . *clack, clack.*
 The grass is as green as a king's front lawn,
    Still wet to the touch when you touch it;
 The morning's so young there's a mist on the field,
    So the light there plays tricks on you such that
You see out in left field, almost in the corner,
    A ball, hooking left, toward the seats

'Til a young Sandy Amorose glides out of nowhere
    And stretches, and leaps, and completes
The catch that the Yankees still can't quite believe . . .
    And before Am'rose lands, there's the sound
Of sharp spikes in the infield that just now was empty
    And you look, and there's Ty Cobb, head down,
Roaring now around second, and heading for third,
    And the third baseman hasn't a prayer,
Because Cobb's coming harder than time or the devil
    With a snarl, and both feet in the air.

And out an the mound, at once sad-eyed and laughing,
    And thumbing his nose now at age
(He struck out major leaguers well into his fifties),
    You're damned if it's not Satchel Paige.
And oddly, as Satchel looks in for the sign
    Old Bill Dickey is flashing his way,
You find your eyes wandering out toward deep center,
    Where Snyder, and Mantle, and Mays
Are each poised to do what each one of them did
    With such grace in those young, dead, gone days.

Go on, *choose* your own heroes from the dugout's top step,
    From the times you're most comfortable in:
At short, Marty Marion, Tony Fernandez;
    In the outfield, Mel Ott, Tony Gwynn.
If you're too young to summon a flying Pete Reiser,
    Then picture the rookie Fred Lynn.
Do it now, while the mist is still thick in the ballpark,
    before the sun burns it away
And begins the next season of all our new moments . . .
    Good morning, it's Opening Day.

SMALL TREASURES

I'm not sure it's actually easier to write badly about sports than it is to write badly about politics or science or literature, but sometimes it feels that way. My students' papers are full of the predictable clichés of sportscasting, of course: "These guys came to play;" "If they lose, there'll be no tomorrow;" "It was a team of destiny." Stuff like that.

But even after they've shed the influence of TV, there is the difficulty of bringing some sense of perspective to the games which so many people take so seriously. Recently, a student wrote that "only sports have the power to astonish us."

"Come on," I scribbled in the margin. "*Only* sports?"

But often enough to keep me teaching, somebody comes up with an image or a line or even a whole paper that is stunning. Just the other day, a second semester freshman wrote about dropping a pass thrown right at him in the closing minutes of a football game last fall. His team was only a couple of points behind at the time. If he had caught the pass, they would have had the lead, and winning would have meant a share of the league championship.

But with a writer's intuition, this young man didn't go on about missing the playoffs, or choking, or letting the team down. Instead, he described himself standing alone in the endzone, looking in disbelief at his hands. He wrote: "My hands didn't catch the ball."

Reading the piece, I felt that — while the crowd roared and the bands played and the coaches feverishly strategized — this unhappy tight end was trying to figure out how to cast off those traitorous, alien hands, hurl them away from himself somehow.

In the same class, another student wrote about riding one of those old, yellow, much-too-small school buses to an away soccer game. He was a tall kid, and he described having to sit with his legs tucked up against the metal back of the seat in front of him with such poignance and precision that when I read it, my own knees ached.

In some classes I've seen remarkable writing from the fan's perspective, too.

Last summer, a student* wrote about going into labor one October night at Fenway Park, timing her contractions by the clock next to the scoreboard, trying to determine whether she could stay for the end of the game. It was a funny, touching, beautifully realized moment.

Later in the paper she wrote:

> *A new life began that October night, but it was also a time of ending. Summer and baseball were over. So was my youth. Babies are never again as portable and well-behaved as when they are unborn. It's not so easy to get to Fenway Park anymore. My husband and I waited for our second child at home, in the winter, when the bleachers and box seats at Fenway were covered with snow, and the metal doors had been pulled tightly down over the entrance gates.*

A treasure like that'll keep me reading student sportswriting for a while.

↰

* Editor's note: Linda Ryan, who later became a commentator for "Only A Game."

SIC TRANSIT GLORIA

The first time I met Al Nipper, he was the center of attention at Fenway Park, because he was about to pitch against Tom Seaver, then of the Chicago White Sox. Rookies pitch against veterans all the time, but the Nipper-Seaver match-up was a good story, because Al Nipper had let everyone know that Tom Seaver had been his idol; that when Nipper was a child, he used to sneak into the ballpark to watch Seaver pitch.

I stood in a knot of reporters and listened that evening as Al Nipper said that after the game he'd probably go looking for Seaver, and he hoped maybe Seaver would give him an autograph. A few minutes after we'd finished, a radio reporter reapproached Nipper sheepishly and said, "Uh, Al, my tape recorder wasn't turned on. Could we go through how thrilling this is, again?"

And without so much as a snarl, Nipper began at the beginning and bubbled enthusiastically until the reporter had all the tape he needed. Nipper had won fewer than 10 games total then; he'd been in the big leagues less than a year.

Over the next few years with the Red Sox, Al Nipper's performances were regularly preceded by the adjective "gutsy," as in "Nipper pitched a gutsy game." That meant he'd given up a dozen or so hits, but gotten a decent hitter on a ground ball when he had to.

Maybe the highlight of his career with Boston was the World Series game he got to start against the Mets. He lasted six and a third innings and lost the game. But he was so thoroughly overmatched on paper by that Mets team that lots of writers still called the outing "gutsy."

Over the years, I spoke with Al Nipper a number of times, usually finding him more accessible than most players. And more thoughtful, too. He shed the goofy, star-struck quality pretty quickly, but he remained a good interview: he was as thoughtful and smart as you'd expect that someone with limited tools would have to be to hold onto the job.

Then, one spring training day not long ago I found myself in need of someone to talk to about the Red Sox, and there was Al Nipper finishing a solitary workout, and he said, sure, he'd talk for a while after he'd showered. So I waited outside the clubhouse with a friend, playing catch in the late afternoon sun, spending time about as pleasantly as it can be spent, until Al Nipper finally came out the door.

"Al," I said. "Hey, Al!" He must have heard me, but he never acknowledged it . . . just jogged to his fast car, hopped in, and drove away in a shower of gravel and dust.

"Well, gee," I joked with my friend later, "it's one thing to be stiffed by Jim Rice or Roger Clemens, but to be stiffed by Al Nipper. Maybe it's time to find another line of work."

Last winter, the Red Sox traded Nipper to the Cubs, and in Chicago his record fell two more games below .500. The other day, I read that elbow and knee injuries may finish him before the '89 season begins. If he's cut, it won't make the headlines. But in the transition from the excited kid, who'd talk for as long as he could, to the bored veteran, who peeled past a patient commentator at Chain o' Lakes Park, he probably represents the Major League ride as well as anyone.

It ain't all glamour. That's the message, I guess.

Sic transit gloria, Al. And not all that much *gloria*.

If it's all over, good luck.

THE BEST INTERESTS OF THE GAME

In the best interests of the game, daytime baseball should be restored on weekdays. This would mean interpreting the phrase *best interests of the game* in some context other than something strictly economic, so it will never happen. But if you've ever skipped work or cut class to watch a Tuesday afternoon ballgame in the sunshine, you know that this activity is not only in the best interests of baseball, but also in the best interests of everyone fortunate enough to be along for the ride.

In the best interests of the game, all the ballparks without grass should be torched . . . Except the carpet wouldn't burn, would it? It would just sort of melt into acrid, indestructible goo. So, maybe the owners of baseball stadiums should be required to trade their ballparks to the owners of football teams, where the outrage would go unnoticed. Footballs bounce funny, no matter what surface they land upon. But baseball . . . watch a game in Kansas some time. Royals Stadium is reputedly a wonderful spot, but not for baseball. It isn't in the best interests of the game when a flyball hitting in front of an outfielder can bounce 12 feet over his head.

In the best interests of baseball, fans engaging in the wave should be given a stern warning, then ejected from the park at their second offense. The game is the show. Along the same lines, then, the San Diego Chicken and all his idiotic brethren or sistren should be driven out. Football is the place for mascots, whether animal or humanoid. It needs all the caged tigers, rooting hogs, and slithering 'gators it can get to keep the crowd amused. Baseball doesn't need giant chickens or Phillie Phanatics. Children who come to the ballpark to see animals are better off watching Ninja Turtles on TV, and the argument that sideshows help develop an audience overlooks the shallowness of the audience which sideshows develop. All of which is another way of saying that — in the best interests of baseball — the game should be played only before initiates and true believers. For the others there is pro wrestling; there is demolition derby.

In the best interests of the game, the schedule should be cut by at least eight games, probably more. It is not in the best interests of the game for pitchers to pitch and hitters to hit in the freezing rain of early April or the snow of late October, no matter how much revenue the long season and the extended playoffs might generate.

In the best interests of the game, the All-Star Game and at least half of the post-season games should occur at a time when people with day jobs can watch them to completion. And it would be nice if kids could see these games live, too, instead of having to watch them on the VCR at breakfast, because they didn't end until after midnight.

In the best interests of the game, there should be a limit as to how many times a manager or player can repeat the same cliché in response to a writer's question. That way, whenever the player says, "It seems it's somebody new picking us up each day," the writer could respond, "I'm sorry, you've said that 12 times this week. You'll have to come up with something else."

And, of course, it's only fair that the writer and broadcasters should have to work under the same rules. A player who was asked about his hamstring more than 12 times in a week would be within his rights if he limited questions to

47

other parts of his anatomy. "Ask me about my thumbs," he might say. "They're all right. And my nose is swell, too!"

Finally, in the best interests of the game, the sports page, as well as sports segments on TV and commentary such as this, should be free of discussion of lawyers, agents, and the inclinations of various players to carry guns, take drugs, or otherwise mess up. Discussions of such matters should be left to the business and crime writers, who need have no concern at all for the best interests of the game.

⚑

OPENING DAY, 1989

They seem stupid as stones sometimes, don't they? Dumb as dirt.
   Or some of them. And we shake our heads and wonder
  Did the gods, with some cosmic or comic balance in mind,
     divert
    Intelligence elsewhere, electing not to pair it with the thunder

In this one's bat, or the whip and snap of that one's arm?
   And then the imp asks us, and we hide the smile,
  "What would you trade, then? What harm
    Would you endure . . . to strike out the side or hit the ball a
     mile?"

If the devil said, "Take five batting titles, or six, or ten,
   And more money than you will ever need:
  But the tradeoff is this . . . again and again,
    You'll tell your whole life in the papers — anyone who can
     read —

And even those who can't, and only watch the dots dance on TV
   Will know each word you ever whispered to your lover,
  Each place you ever kissed her, each degree
    Of each angle of descent, each lie you used to cover

Up one from the other or the other from the one —
   These are private things that keep your fans from sleep
  On nights when they are lost, and cannot run,
    Don't know which name to whisper in the dark and deep —

49

But their griefs, at least are private, their griefs, their own;
    And yours will be a source of dirty jokes.
  Or this: "I'll give you," says the devil, "more hits than
      anyone,
    And not just bingles — leg doubles, too, and longer pokes

And fire to see you through the years, and such acclaim . . .
    As no one since Ty Cobb has ever known.
  But it won't heal you, or delight you — you'll be the same
    As Cobb, who died fighting the electric bill, and died
      alone."

Here is the challenge for the crowd, wrapped from the boxes
    to the cheap seats —
    There's dismay in the dugout, bad blood in the locker
    room and the hotel;
  What will we bring to it, this pleasing game that meets
    Us each April, and sings and carries through our summers
    so well?

We're not novices here, We weren't born yesterday.
    We've suffered the president who thought he could call
    the missiles back.
  "I am not a crook," I heard another say . . .
    And then he quit — with the election process still intact.

Likewise, today we'll be all right, we'll shrug it aside —
    No problem. The charges and the counter-charges,
    gambling, lying, cheating,
  Bedroom or boardroom folly, each sad or silly ride,
    The old heart of the summer game's still beating;

No player's foolishness or worse, finally, does much
    But spice the rich broth that sustains us on our way;
  And finally the dumbest, dirtiest stories, though they touch
    Us, give us pause, won't keep us from the ballpark
    Opening Day.

POSTPONING SURRENDER

The shift to daylight savings time, the light of summer, brings out the fast-pitch softball teams again. You'll see them gathering and stretching on every neighborhood field in Boston from now until September.

Some teams are made up of high school kids. They warm up like the Harlem Globe Trotters. They dress in new, white doubleknit uniforms, just like the pros wear. They sling the ball around the infield as if their arms will last forever. Somewhere, moving deliberately in the blur of their activity, there will be a pitcher who's at least 40. There doesn't seem to be any such thing as a young, fast-pitch softball pitcher.

The teams which are not made up of kids are less flashy, but more interesting. One boasts a couple of lawyers who change out of their suits into sweatpants in their cars and carry baseball gloves in their briefcases with the deeds and depositions. They play for this team which has stayed together for about 15 years, through the predictable ravages of other sports and time.

The second baseman and the centerfielder wear bulky knee braces, the same kind developed for Joe Namath years back. The first baseman hasn't been able to throw naturally since a skiing accident in 1979. When someone on the other team bunts his way, he fields the ball and flips it underhanded to the catcher, who fires it to the second baseman covering first. Most teams made up of high school kids will beat a team that uses a cut-off man fielding a bunt.

This team plays on fields where children have been riding their motorbikes, throwing rocks, digging holes, and playing with their dogs all day. The presiding umpires sort of tune in and tune out the essentials of the game, depending on how loudly someone is shouting at them. On one particularly battered field, the ump is consistently so loaded by seven o'clock or so that both sides generally agree to disregard his decisions and determine balls and strikes on their own.

The crowd in the wooden bleachers is likely to be small — pretty much the long-suffering, immediate families of a few players. The lights are sometimes so bad you can lose track of a slow ground ball in the shadows.

Still, there is seriousness of purpose here, amid the random chatter, the howling of babies, the jingle of the ice cream truck, and the summer hum of radios. There is the common goal of winning, of course, because without that there'd be no game. But now, as daylight saving begins and the new schedule gets underway, there's the more fundamental recognition that they've all showed up to begin again. They've postponed for one more season, at least, the surrender to golf, weekend tennis, or lemonade on the porch.

"Constantly risking absurdity," they're still on their toes in the dust of the playgrounds, pounding their gloves, taking their cuts, eyes on the ball.

THE BASEBALL ENCYCLOPEDIA

In his last season, Luis Tiant's father went 10-0 with the New York Cubans. He may have been 41 years old, as the birthdate next to his name indicates. In any case, he had a splendid sense of timing. How many of us will be able to say we were undefeated in our last season when the time comes?

Some of the statistics and small print facts in this book tell stories.

Willie Mays was once traded for Charlie Williams and $50,000.

In one calendar year, Dave Kingman went from the New York Mets to San Diego for Bobby Valentine and Paul Siebert, then to California for cash, then to the Yankees for cash, and then to the White Sox for nothing.

Roger Maris was once traded for Marv Throneberry.

Chicago won the National League pennant in 1876 with one pitcher, Al Spalding (47-13), who also managed the club.

Cool Papa Bell played for 25 years in the Negro Leagues, at least as far as anyone has been able to determine. He spent five years playing in Mexico and the Dominican Republic. *The Baseball Encyclopedia* doesn't have the stats for franchises there.

In 1962, the Mets had two pitchers named Bob Miller. The one who was 2-2 probably hated being confused with the one who was 1-12.

It is true that Moonlight Graham played in one game in the big leagues and never got to hit. Peaches Graham, on the other hand, hit .265 over several seasons with Cleveland, Chicago, Boston, and Philadelphia.

Barney Graham, Bernie Graham, Skinny Graham, and Tiny Graham also saw big league action. It's sort of remarkable that none of them was nicknamed "Candy."

This is a book to be celebrated for various reasons, and since its first edition came out several decades ago, I've only encountered one reason to wish it hadn't.

There was this old guy who used to umpire in the softball league I play in. (We'll call him Bud.) A couple of years ago he was entertaining some young players after a game with tales of his exploits in the big leagues.

"I played for Jimmy Dykes," he said. "I was on some pretty good White Sox teams. I played against Gehrig and DiMaggio."

"Jeez," somebody said, "you musta seen Connie Mack."

"Absolutely," Bud told him. "Course he was an old man by then; older than I am now."

He went on for a while about Hank Greenberg and Mickey Cochrane and Lefty Gomez, and I made a note of his name. I went home after the game that night and looked him up in *The Baseball Encyclopedia*, and — of course — he wasn't there. The book's only existed since 1969. Before then, Bud would have gotten away with his stories. Who'd have had the time or the energy or even the inclination to look it up before that process became so easy?

At the next game, a guy on my team who knew I was going to check on Bud asked me about it. I told him there was no record of anybody by that name ever playing for the White Sox or anyone else.

"Oh, well," he said, "what the hell." Then he picked up a ball, and we went out toward right field to warm up. That was the only time I sort of wished they hadn't come up with *The Baseball Encyclopedia*.

THE LIMITS OF SCIENCE

Recently, a scientist from somewhere sent me an article that says a *curve ball* doesn't curve. Most months when I don't get such an article in the mail, I get one that talks about how the *rising fastball* is a misnomer, because a ball thrown overhand can't rise. According to these articles the ball can't hop, slide, or hiss, either, though most acknowledge grudgingly that it might sink just a little.

I love these articles for a lot of reasons. They are so solemn, most of them, and so fierce. And — of course — they are so wrong.

This is not to say that I don't believe that science has its place, because it certainly does. Science is good for naming plants and pinning down the age of rocks. Scientists have developed astonishing ways to cure sick people one at a time and spectacular ways to kill healthy people in great numbers all at once.

But these attempts to apply science — in this case Physics — to baseball always remind me of the doctors of a bygone era who would try to prove the existence of the soul by weighing their patients just before and just after they died. In life and in baseball, there are certain matters which we must accept on faith. Especially in baseball.

One of these is that for well over a century now — from

the days of Cy Young up through the era of Christy Mathewson and into the time of Bob Gibson and the present of Bert Blyleven, Roger Clemens, and Charlie Hough — our culture has produced a number of fellows with the ability to make a baseball spin, sing, hum, turn left or right (apparently on command), and drop like lead in a well out of the spot where we just (*Damn!*) saw it not a tenth of a second ago.

The scientists say that the waist-high fastball which suddenly nicks your chin only *appears* to rise, because it does not fall as far as you anticipate that it will. The scientists say that the ball that is right there for you and then is suddenly pulling the catcher out toward first base (while you lurch after it with your tail in the air) only *seems* to curve.

But I know differently, and many of you do, too. Let me speak for all of us on this, empirically and with conviction.

If that baseball did not spin, sing, hum, turn left or right upon command, curve (yes, curve *and* rise), too . . . If it did not do those things, I would not be a teacher, and a writer, and a radio commentator. Because if that baseball did not do those things, I would be a hitter.

ß

TOSSING A GAMER

Rob Murphy is a relief pitcher whose chief claim to notoriety is the resilience of his left arm. His first four years in the big leagues resulted in an unremarkable won-lost record of 19-18. He saved a modest 16 games. But from 1987 through 1989 he *appeared* in 237 games: first for the Reds; then, for the Red Sox. During that stretch no pitcher worked more often. This meant that on each day which his team played, Rob Murphy had to assume that he would pitch, even if only to a batter or two. Maybe this perpetual state of anticipation accounts for Rob Murphy's belief in superstition. And therein lies the tale.

When the Cleveland Indians rallied to beat the Red Sox on Saturday night, Murphy angrily tossed his glove into the crowd as he left the field. Assuming that Murphy had acted without thinking and would want his old glove back, the man who caught it initally offered to trade it for a new glove. Given how attached most ballplayers become to their gloves, it was a logical offer.

Lots of major leaguers are superstitious about the food they eat, about who touches their bats, about how many times they tap their spikes before stepping in to face a pitcher. But the mystique associated with the glove with which a fellow takes the field — his *gamer* — is as strong as any in sports. It is the tool with which he protects himself from the ball, and from the unparalleled humiliation of the lonely, naked error. A good glove becomes not just an essential tool, but the familiar extension of a man's hand.

But Murphy had no interest in retrieving this particular extension.

"Okay," the guy in the stands told a reporter. "Tell him he can have the glove back if he'll buy me a lobster dinner the next time I'm in Boston."

But the fan just didn't get it. Murphy didn't *want* the glove back . . . didn't ever want to see it again . . . believed it was full of bad pitches. Nor was it the first time he'd acted on such a conviction by casting the offending mitt away from him. After a loss a couple of years ago, he tossed a glove into the stands in St. Louis. An obliging woman retrieved it, and Murphy found it in his locker the next day.

"I threw it in the trash," he said, "but when I came to the park the next day it was in my locker again. Then we flew to Chicago, and it turned up in my locker there. It turned out Dave Concepcion had seen me throwing it away, and he kept sneaking it out of the garbage and returning it."

So far, this time around the offending glove has stayed gone. In his first appearance after tossing the thing into the seats, Rob Murphy used the mitt of reserve outfielder Danny Heep, who must have been rooting even harder than usual for a decent performance by the reliever.

Reminded by reporters of the enormous market for baseball memorabilia of all kinds (a market in which a glove that had seen action — even *ignominious* action — in a major league game would be worth plenty), Murphy was unmoved. As far as he's concerned, the man who retrieved his mitt has no prize.

"It's not worth a *bleep*," Rob Murphy was heard to say in Cleveland Sunday. "More power to the guy who caught it. All that I hope is that he doesn't try to pitch."

☞

ALIENS

This spring, I was an assistant coach with the Needham, Massachusetts Aliens, a collection of nine-year-old girls which earned its nickname during the first practice when several of the young athletes picked up the orange cones we'd used to mark the sidelines and began running up and down the field with them on their heads. Aliens.

My chief contribution to the team was minimal: a mid-season suggestion to the head coach and the other assistant that perhaps we should stop shouting contradictory instructions at the players, at least during the games.

Probably for reasons other than that, the Aliens enjoyed a successful campaign. Everybody played each position, the team improved consistently, and the Aliens even won a post-season tournament and got trophies, which — as far as my daughter was concerned — was the highlight of her soccer career.

My own candidate for "highlight" came earlier in Amy's soccer days, though, on a day that she may not even remember. Last year, as an even less experienced assistant coach, I watched her play for a team that didn't win any trophies. It was also a team on which none of the girls ever wanted to play goalie. The two circumstances may have been related.

Anyway, moments before one particular game, the coach designated one of Amy's teammates the starting goalie and pointed toward the goal she would be tending. The little girl burst into tears and ran in the opposite direction. These things happen among eight-year-old soccer players. With no prompting, Amy stepped forward and said, "I'll be goalie."

She didn't like playing goalie. She'd told me that. But to the relief of her coach and her teammates, she trotted out to the position so the game could begin.

At the half, Amy's team was up one. Still, nobody else wanted to play goalie. When the game ended — with Amy still in goal — they were down one.

As we walked to the car, I said, "I'm proud of you."

"We lost," she said.

"You played a good game," I said, "and you took the girl who was crying off the hook."

She shrugged. "Can I have a friend over?" she asked.

It is said that sports builds character. It may be true. But for this neophyte coach, this father who always seems to be saying to his daughter, "Enough with the smart mouth," or "Clean up your room," the more important function of that game was to provide the reminder that the character was already there.

ß

TOO MUCH SPORTS

We watched the pro hockey in L.A. and Pittsburgh,
  In Edmonton, and in D.C.
And, of course, up in Boston, although not in Austin,
  And Chicago got upset, I see.
But Chi's got the Bulls, and the Cubs, and the White Sox,
  And they're all in action this week.
And the Mets and the Yanks and the Knicks are still at it,
  So there's no time in New York for sleep.
The Pistons, the Sonics, the Blazers, the Rockets,
  The Lakers, the Jazz, and the Hawks,
Compete for tube time with the Tigers, the Mariners,
  Astros, and Dodgers, and squawks
Of "Too much!" will, alas, go unheeded,
  As long as the money rolls in,
For the Padres and Angels, the Bucks and the Reds,
  And each millionaire Twin Cities Twin
Who will play in the glare of the shining North Stars,
  While the Timber Wolves howl in dismay,
That their season is over — Gosh, how can *that* be
  At only the onset of May?
But take heart, there's still roundball in Indy, and
  Phoenix, Milwaukee, and Philly and more,
And football in Raleigh, and London, and Frankfort,
  Though not yet in San Salvador.

61

Though it's only a matter of time, I suppose,
    Before hockey, and football and hoop,
  Head down into Mexico, through Guatemala, and south
    To complete a great loop
Of *true* world-wide games, how far off can it be?
    Until World Leagues sprout up in each sport?
And folks who would follow for fun something else,
    Will most likely have to resort
To some other medium — *not* the TV —
    Which will fill up with athletes and thugs
The Ducks and the Field Mice, the Spiders, the Scorpions,
    Maybe the Battling Bugs,
The Owls and the Frogs, the hard-charging Sea Urchins,
    This may sound peculiar, my friends,
But the triple A players who work in Toledo
    Have always been called the Mud Hens,
And with teams in Orlando and Raleigh-slash-Durham,
    And all the sports going full bore
It can't be too long 'til they run out of names and
    Start combing landscape for more.

Meanwhile all the Giants and Astros and Indians,
    Penguins and Oilers and Spurs,
  Will run, jump, and skate as we all go dumb watching
    Them turn into televised blurs.
A metaphor, maybe, for a time we have lost
    When we knew who played what, when, and where.
As it's gotten so hard to keep track of them all,
    It's perhaps gotten harder to care.

INDY

In order to qualify for a recent Indy 500, Emerson Fittipaldi drove his Chevrolet around the most famous race track in the land at an average speed of better than 225 miles per hour.

Let's consider that in layman's terms for a minute: 225 miles per hour is about four times the speed that will get you arrested on an interstate if your part of the country is still collecting enough tax money to employ police officers.

Granted, there are lots of sports which would be hard to explain to someone from another planet. Think about how many hours it would take to even *get* to the infield fly rule, let alone the vagaries of clearing waivers. But the Indianapolis 500 presents difficuties of a more fundamental nature.

"We have been studying your world for some time," the alien might say. "We have noticed that you are burning an ever-larger hole in the atmosphere which surrounds your planet by exploding vast quantities of fossil fuel in these cars which you take with you wherever you go."

"Yes, well, we're working on that," you might answer.

"And then there is this race each spring," the alien might continue. "Around and around they go, whining and roaring, racing to nowhere, really. And the monotony is only broken when someone loses control and careens into the wall. Then everywhere there are howls of dismay and surprise. How could anyone be surprised when this happens at 225 miles per hour?"

"Okay, granted," you might say, "but many more times than not, the drivers walk away from such crashes. The cars are miracles of engineering as they shatter. The drivers almost always live to race another day."

"Very peculiar that they should want to do that, isn't it?" the alien would smile.

Some of our other games give us metaphors for death. In baseball, victory goes to the team that makes it home safely most often. Lots of sports end in ties during regulation time and invoke a format called *sudden death* to resolve the issue. But auto racing — the sport of which the Indianapolis 500 is the centerpiece in this country — is the spectacle of death at once most flamboyant and most naked. Bouncing off a barrier at 200 miles an hour in a ball of flame is not a metaphor for anything.

Auto racing in various forms is the most popular spectator sport in the United States, despite the fact that television pays less attention to it than it does to baseball, basketball, or football, and despite the fact that a close race is a relatively rare event. People are apparently drawn to it as spectacle as much as bv concern for who will win. If you don't believe that, compare the volume of the announcer's voice when he tells us who has finished first with the scream with which he describes four or five drivers trying to avoid a lame car which has spun sideways like an enormous, mobile land mine into the pack.

Maybe baseball tells us about our history, and our affection for that which does not change much. Maybe football tells us about the corporate mentality which our century has developed and the military mindset into which some fall so comfortably, whether there's a war or not. But given the numbers and the stone-simple event which draws them, it's impossible to escape the fact that auto racing has more to tell us about ourselves and what we need than any of our other games. Great crowds of us are for cars and speed and noise and the spice of impending public disaster. Welcome to Indianapolis. Welcome to America.

SPRING TRAINING

It is time for stories of spring training. Actually, it's past time. The stories began appearing a couple of weeks ago, when the first restless players started showing up in Florida or Arizona. Former manager Sparky Anderson, without a spring training destination for the first time in 26 years, sat at home in California, waiting for the phone to ring.

"I'm done," said Sparky, "but *done* is not *never*."

A spring training kind of thing to say if ever there was one.

To be at spring training is a splendid proposition: it's green grass, sunshine, and players and managers more inclined to speak thoughtfully than they are during the regular season. Even in the age of home gyms and personal trainers, Major League Baseball clings to the silly contention that it takes a month and a half of jogging in the outfield and games that don't count to get ready for the six-month season, and God bless the game for that.

But you don't have to be there to need spring training and to love it. Spring training is a state of mind. It is about stretching and standing around the batting cage and laughing at dumb jokes — and then calling it a day. Come to think of it, maybe spring training is best regarded at a distance. On the premises, you're likely to see young men competing for jobs and older men anxiously trying to convince themselves and their employers that they can still help somebody, which is fine when it works and not so good at all when it doesn't. But from a distance it's all flip and pepper, games baseball players play. It's about getting loose.

About ten years ago, in a spring training camp in Florida, I came upon a guy employed by one of the sporting goods companies to peddle gloves to the major leaguers. Two years earlier, he'd been a Triple A player — a kid with a future in the bigs — but he'd gotten hurt, and he'd gotten married, and he'd decided that he'd better go to work. But early on that sunny morning when I met him, somebody on the team that had once seen him as a prospect saw him woefully watching batting practice and invited him to take a few cuts.

"How'd you do?" I asked him.

He looked at me and past me into a future that was gone. He was a salesman now, but his eyes were a hitter's eyes. He smiled.

"I hit nothing but line drives," he said.

Granted Sparky's gift of phraseology, he might have said, "I'm *done*, but done is not *never*."

That's what spring training is for.

꒜

Grapefruit League Afternoon

Last week I took my kids to a ball game. I suppose it was a
case of their humoring me. We'd spent two days at Disney
World. We would spend most of the next day at a place
where you can drive your car among lions and giraffes.

"What the heck?" the kids might have figured . . . "We'll
go along with Dad's idea, go see some baseball."

My wife warned me not to expect too much. "Maybe
they'll last an inning," she said, perhaps hoping.

But the kids surprised her. The game was already in
progress when we took our box seats a few feet to the first
base side of home plate. There was action everywhere in the
tiny, perfect park. The batter took his practice swings, the
pitcher stretched and looked the runner back to first, the
coaches hollered, and the fans whistled and clapped for a rally.

"What's that little boy doing?" asked my older daughter,
Amy, who is four and a half.

"That's the batboy," I said. "He gets the foul balls that
bounce back onto the field off the screen. He takes the
players' bats and helmets back to the dugout when they're
finished with them.

"Look at the pitcher now. See how he's winding up,
getting ready to let one go?"

"When will the little boy be back?" Amy asked.

If she could have had one autograph that day, it would have been the batboy's. But even he was forgotten when the peanut vendor arrived. I bought Amy a bag and watched as she shelled and ate a few nuts, then began looking about uncomfortably. Finally, she turned to her grandmother and asked, "Where do I put the shells?"

I bit my tongue and prayed that Granny would answer that one right.

"Throw 'em on the floor," she smiled, and Amy did, and all was well.

For my younger daughter, too, the ballpark — in this case Municipal Stadium in West Palm Beach — was a fine place. She said "hi" to everyone within range, mostly grandfathers and grandmothers who were thoroughly enchanted. Then she scrambled around picking up the peanut shells which her sister had so happily dropped and put them on the bald head of the man in the seat in front of her so she could watch them slide down into his collar like big bugs. I do not know this man's name, but he will go to heaven when the time comes. He acted as if nothing could be more delightful than to have a 16-month-old child put shells on his head for four innings.

Four innings was it, even though only a run separated the Expos and the Braves in the top of the fifth. I figured it was better to let the image of our first ball game shine in the family's collective memory, unadulterated by tears, pouting, or toddler breakdown.

Whether it worked — whether my daughters have in their dreams now the seed of the love of baseball: its sights and sounds and movements — I don't know. But in the airport a few days later while we waited to board our delayed flight home, Alison, the 16-month-old, threw her milk cup across a row of chairs and hit an old gentleman square in the chest.

"What are you doing," the fellow growled, pretending to be fierce, "Practicing to be a ballplayer?"

So maybe it did.

MASTER TIGER

I was s'posed to go out for the groceries this evening . . .
    I couldn't deliver the goods.
  I was busy (just as I've been busy for days now)
    Thinking of Tiger Woods.

A faucet is dripping, the kids want a snack,
    And the dog needs to go for a walk.
  The sink's full of dishes, the car's out of gas,
    And my wife says that we have to talk.

The yard's full of tree limbs from last week's big storm,
    And my laundry's all over the floor.
  The downspout aims water right into the basement,
    And they say that it's gonna pour.

But how can I worry? And where is the meaning
    Of these dreary tasks and concerns?
  I witnessed for four days on TV from Georgia
    The grace toward which humankind yearns!

Some have their philosophers, poets, and saints
    To define for them shouldn'ts and shoulds.
  Not me, pal. My sign is the swoosh of the Nike;
    My mentor? The great Tiger Woods.

You may say it's early for "great" to apply,
    Or that Tiger's just playing a game.
  I reply that he's greater already than any
    Phenomenon that you can name.

At twenty-one he's won a hallowed green jacket.
    He ate up the Masters for lunch.
  But that's just the start. He's much bigger than sports,
    And I say this though it's just a hunch:

He's bigger than all of the Beatles together.
    He dwarfs the Colossus of Rhodes.
  His gaze is hypnotic, his touch can cure lepers,
    And heal warts you've gotten from toads.

His breath is all peppermint. He has no cavities.
    Birds never spatter his car.
  He's all of the myst'ries of hist'ry resolved,
    And he shoots about 12 under par.

So, bother me not with such worries as work, or
    Relationships, chattel, or goods.
  From now on I spend my life free of all thoughts
    But the perfect, supreme Tiger Woods.

⚑

RELICS

A Christy Mathewson card shows the great New York pitcher not in uniform, but in an impossibly uncomfortable-looking high collar, bow tie slightly askew, glaring into some middle-distant immortality. "Pitcher of the New York Club," reads the caption. That's a little like identifying John Geilgud as an actor with an English accent. Anyway, the Mathewson card can probably be had for between $5,000 and $6,000.

How about an autographed photograph album which includes a picture of Kid Gleason, manager of the White Sox team that tanked the Series in 1919? To his credit, Kid's looking right at the camera, as if daring any of us to conclude that he was mixed-up in the fix. The whole album will probably go for between eight and ten grand, which is more than all but two of the eight fixers got for their efforts 72 years ago.

For Boston fans there is a Carl Yastrzemski game jersey. There's also a 1954 Ted Williams baseball card with a package of hot dogs in the upper left hand corner. It's sort of a strange, unintentional gag card, the effect of which is to leave one wondering how Ted could have concentrated on his follow through while some crazed fan was trying to bean him with about 45 pounds of franks. Anyway it's mint and available for five to six thousand.

All these things and more will be auctioned at the

Fairmount Hotel in San Francisco, and part of the appeal will be in the stories you can imagine behind the prizes. What catastrophe could have induced Fred Lindstrom's heirs to part with his Hall of Fame induction award at any price? Who is the '69 Met who pawned his World Series ring? And how would he feel to know it's expected to bring about $12,000 now? The intrinsic charm of most of the items is obvious enough (at least to the sort of folks who collect baseball odds and ends), but there are a few mysteries in the lot.

There's a baseball signed by five guys who were either league presidents or commissioners of the game. Who'd want the autographs of a bunch of pompous executives — whatever business they happened to be running — unless the signatures were on checks?

There are plenty of other uniform jerseys besides Carl Yastrzemski's, shirts worn by such luminaries as Warren Spahn, Willie Mays, Jackie Robinson, and Nolan Ryan. My favorite is Casey Stengal's home jersey from one of his seasons managing the hopeless Mets of the mid-60s. It looks like somebody has spilled scrambled eggs all over the front of it. My guess is that they're authentic eggs, authentically served to Casey, who authentically fumbled them all over the place and into posterity. The auctioneers figure the shirt, stains included, will bring in $15,000.

If you've got that sort of cash burning a hole in your pocket, it might be worth a trip to San Francisco. The Giants or the A's will be home. You could see a game while you're there. Even box seats will feel like a bargain in this context. Save your program and your ticket stub. And take solace from the fact that some part of the proceeds from this extravaganza will go into a fund which helps out former ballplayers in need, meaning that a trickle of the loot that changes hands may eventually find its way to some of the guys who had to let this neat stuff go.

ß

ONE FANTASY PRESERVED

A friend of mine who is a serious, long-time baseball fan decided years ago that he would never witness spring training.

This is not because he doesn't like to travel. He's been to Australia and New Zealand. He's been to Europe a couple of times. He's watched games in major league ballparks on both coasts and at a lot of minor league parks in between.

But he does not go to spring training. He says that he's afraid that if he did, the reality of that celebrated phenomenon — no matter how splendid — would fail to live up to the ideal of March baseball which be has carried in his head and in his heart for thirty-odd years.

Like me, this friend lives in a city where March is less likely to serve as a harbinger of spring than it is to rot your shoes. Even on Opening Day up here, fans with brains bring down jackets and woolen hats to the ballpark. So spring training for my friend has always been something far away and a little unreal, and he prefers to keep it that way. In his vision of what is going on now in Fort Myers and Lakeland and Vero Beach, all is limbering up on clipped grass under a perfect sky. He has heard about spring training, of course, and read about it, but as long as the players have not snapped at the writers in March in his presence, it might as well not have happened.

73

In his vision there is no place for the cranky holdout pitcher or the ambulance parked alongside the bleacher for the old Tiger fan who falters in the climb to his seat. There are no baffled grandfathers in the parking lot trying to explain to their clinging grandsons and granddaughters that the game they've come to see has been sold out for a month. There are no traffic jams, no sunburned noses, and no stretches of hot highway where only the Kentucky Frieds and the Taco Bells break the monotony of the Burger Kings. There is only baseball in his vision, and it is daytime, outdoor baseball in which nobody gets hurt, and the point of it all is the game rather than the salaries or the revenue the town takes in or even the score.

I don't exactly envy my friend this vision. I've seen 12 or 15 spring training games over the years, and I've enjoyed almost all of them a lot. But I don't dream about spring training anymore, so I envy my friend's tenacity. I admire the determination with which he holds on to an old and happy idea of the game in Florida in March as it once was. Or, perhaps, as it never was.

He knows the value of a dream, this friend of mine . . . how necessary it is, and how rare, and how fragile.

R

Baseball 101

One of the college's librarians introduced me to Sergei last week. He is one of 35 scholars visiting from the Soviet Union to study, as well as to teach culture and language here in the United States.

"He wants to learn baseball," the librarian said. "I thought maybe you could help."

So, I told Sergei to meet me out on the ballfield in the morning.

We were there before it was hot. Nobody plays on this field after school's out in the spring, but someone had groomed it anyway. There were no baselines, but the dirt had been rolled recently, and the grass was clipped and green.

"It's beautiful," Sergei said.

"That's a good start," I told him.

I gave him a glove and a ball, and we had a catch. I waved him toward the infield and tapped a couple of grounders at him. Then I gave him the bat, stood him at the plate, and threw him a couple of pitches. "Don't swing at anything that isn't over the plate and between the letters and the knees," I told him.

"Why not?" he asked.

"Ted Williams says not to," I said.

"Who is Ted Williams?" he said.

"That's lesson two," I said.

We repaired to my office, where I showed him a picture of Williams shaking hands with Babe Ruth. I showed him the photo sequence of Willie Mays' catch in the '54 World Series and then brought out the issue of *The Sporting News* that shows Mays on his last day in uniform — great forever, but bewildered — seeking in the camera lens some clue to where the glory has gone.

"He is sad," Sergei said.

"Yes, he is," I agreed, "because he played the outfield as well an anyone ever has. And he hit with joy. He couldn't wait to hit. But when that picture was taken he was 42, and he couldn't do any of it worth a damn anymore. By then, sometimes he would start after a ball and fall down."

"But there is always another young man coming along," Sergei said.

"Yes, indeed," I said. "You're on to one of the truths of baseball now. The team in Boston just signed a fellow named Rodriguez who pitches and plays shortstop. He throws over 90 miles an hour, but he doesn't want to be just a pitcher. He loves the game so much he wants to play every day."

"Boston," Sergei said. "Boston is the Red Sox."

"Yes," I said.

"Well," he said, "I am beginning to understand baseball: the throwing, the catching, and the hitting. And I am beginning to see the sadness of Willie Mays when he is 42 and the joy of this Rodriguez, who is only a boy. But this Boston Red Sox . . . I still don't understand this Boston Red Sox. Why do they never win?"

Behind me on the shelf with *The Baseball Encyclopedia* were a few items more likely to be familiar to my guest. I pulled out *The Bible* marked at "The Book of Job." I reached for *Crime and Punishment* and *King Lear*.

"Sergei," I said, "where do you want to begin?"

⅊

OPENING DAY, 1993

It should be sun-splashed, warm and promising,
    Blue skies overhead.
It should echo with shouts and laughter,
    And hope should rise like bread.
There should be a seat for every child
    Who's never been to a game,
And the home team should win in each park today,
    No matter the home team's name.

The rookie who barely made the club
    Should go three for four with a walk;
The old guy back on a surgical knee
    Should steal third and get home on a balk.
The beer should be cold and the hot dogs hot,
    And the popcorn and peanuts free . . .
And no one should even consider the wave,
    Or watching replays on TV.

The pitchers should work without delay,
    And the hitters should step in and hit,
The umpires should be so sure on their calls
    That no one gives them . . . a hard time.

It won't be that way, not in every park,
    Not in any park, I suppose.
Instead, the traffic will pile up early,
    And in the cheap seats the bozos

Will rip off their shirts, though it's forty degrees
   And scream at the players below.
The reliever who cost the home team untold millions
   Will struggle, and probably blow
The save, and the manager, tired already,
   Will trudge like slow death to the mound,
And the kids will be restive and angry and cold,
   And the pitcher will stare at the ground.

The visiting team will score often and easily,
   Turning the game to a rout.
By the fourth, half the crowd will have left in disgust,
   Their summer now riddled with doubt.

We go because we don't know which it will be,
   And because, against sense, we still care.
We go to be back in the presence of baseball,
   To witness it, because it's there.
We go to renew that corn-pone continuity
   Some of us value, and, hey,
We go because fading and loss notwithstanding,
   Each year still has Opening Day.

℞

HANK AARON

Twenty years after the fact, Hank Aaron still remembers that everybody in the ballpark that April night in 1975 when he finally broke Babe Ruth's record was cold, but he wasn't.

He remembers that Jimmy Carter, then Governor of Georgia, was at the game.

He remembers that he wanted to get the chase behind him, because for a year or so the number of media folks following him and his teammates from city to city had been growing larger and larger. By the time Aaron hit his 715th homerun, the Atlanta locker room was always so cluttered with reporters and cameramen that there was scarcely room for the Braves to change their clothes. Aaron remembers that he felt bad for his teammates.

It is significant that in this week's teleconference marking the anniversary of dinger number 715, Mr. Aaron was not inclined to talk about the witless insults and death threats that came daily then from the people who could not stand the idea that the Black Aaron would break the record of the great Ruth. Henry Aaron ignored the distractions and worse as he methodically hacked away at each day's pitcher, gradually gaining ground on and then moving beyond one of baseball's most enduring standards.

There are those who say that the most remarkable feature

of Hank Aaron's career was the consistency that characterized it. In 23 years, he hit more than 44 home runs only once (45 in 1962), but he hit fewer than 20 only three times. He whacked nearly 3800 hits and drove in almost 2300 runs. But these are only baseball achievements, as are all the homers.

More remarkable, I think, was the quiet determination which drove Hank Aaron through the taunts and threats and dumb wondering whether Aaron's 715th home run would magically erase from the public imagination the very image of Babe Ruth.

Of course, that did not happen. Home run number 715 — and the 44 more that followed it out of various ballparks over the next few years — did nothing to diminish Ruth's mythical presence, though they did, of course, enhance Hank Aaron's achievement.

And perhaps they did more. Though it shouldn't have been necessary as recently as 20 years ago, Hank Aaron's record-breaking home run took its place beside the many knockout victories of Jack Johnson and Joe Louis, the gold medals of Jesse Owens and Wilma Rudolph, and the MVP award that Jackie Robinson won in 1949.

When Hank Aaron began hitting home runs for the Braves, the major leagues had been integrated for less than a decade. When he nailed number 715, the freedom marches and civil rights legislation of the 60s were old news. But the taunts and the death threats came anyway, while Hank Aaron went about his hammering. And he, too, overcame.

ᚦ

ARTHUR ASHE

In the business of talking and writing about athletes and their games, we overstate things more often than not. We are caught up so frequently in momentary triumphs or last minute losses that it is hard to write about somebody who avoided that snare and made a life characterized by serenity and purpose rather than hoopla.

As a tennis player, Arthur Ashe was a pure joy to watch. He was a hard hitter, but his power seemed to come from the fact that he'd eliminated wasted motion from his stroke. He was a craftsman rather than a showman. There were no grunts, and there was no racket tossing. While other players offered the crowd histrionics, Ashe offered elegant tennis. Whenever he won, you had the feeling that form and function had become one, and that justice and righteousness had been served.

But that was only the beginning. When he fought against the vicious and stupid apartheid system in South Africa, he did so as a thoughtful, independent man. Committed to the cause of equal rights and courageous in the fight to bring that goal closer, Ashe was also sensitive to those who felt he chose the wrong tactic when he elected to play tennis in South Africa in order to give his brothers a champion with whom they could identify. Ashe respected and listened to his critics.

He never closed his mind to tactics other than his own. But he seemed always to know who he was and what he could do. He brought the same energy and the same serenity to his work as an educator when he talked to audiences about AIDS.

In sports, a sprained ankle that keeps somebody out of the playoffs is often described as a tragedy. Arthur Ashe suffered several heart attacks, underwent surgery several times, became infected with HIV as a result of a blood transfusion, and still maintained his concentration, his determination, and his wit. He died too young, of course, before his child could grow up. His death is the kind of circumstance that leads some to curse fate or God.

But his life was a marvel of energy and commitment against the considerable odds of racism and other forms of intolerance within the context of his sport and well beyond it. His life is cause for celebration.

$$\sim$$

SUMMER

SUMMER MAIL

My favorite press release this week comes from the people at the Volvo International Tennis Tournament, who have taken time out to inform me that they are already accepting ticket orders for the 1989 tournament, the '88 Volvo International having sold out some months ago. So *ha, ha* and tough luck to those of you who thought you were going to see pro tennis in Vermont this summer. I suppose those of us who missed out will somehow muddle through.

There's a note, too, from the Myopia Hunt Club, a place where they play polo on Sundays during the summer. The fun in getting their releases is in the names of the people who write them and send them; names which always work backwards as well as forwards. I wonder if that's somehow characteristic of polo playing families? This week's entry comes from Brenda Bronson and Surrey Jay. Brenda Bronson, Bronson Brenda. Surrey Jay, Jay Surrey. See what I mean?

I got a t-shirt in the mail this week from a company that's promoting a phone service which enables sports fans in Boston to call a 900 number 24-hours-a-day and get a complete sports wrap up. Their hook was the opportunity to hear a blow-by-blow description of the Tyson-Spinks fight, but I didn't open the mail until that opportunity had passed. Too bad. It would have been a cheap call.

Anyway, the t-shirt has a bunch of athletes talking on the phone on the front, and the number you should call for scores on the back. By wearing it, then, I'd become an advertisement for this service for gamblers. That's not something I'd necessarily mind, I suppose, but there was no check in the package the t-shirt came in, and I'm not going to promote this business for free. I urge the same attitude on all of you out there wearing shirts featuring the logos of sneaker companies, breweries, and Walt Disney World. If you're gonna shill for those megaliths, at least make them pay.

I got a book in the mail this week, too. It purports to tell the "behind the scenes story of the pro football draft" from 1936 to the present. First listener to send a self-addressed envelope with sufficient postage receives a book.

Finally, a toy company sent me a little plastic Wade Boggs doll, resplendent in a Red Sox home uniform, bat cocked. You can move his little head, shoulders, and waist, in case Boggs decides to change the stance that has brought him three batting titles. The former pro football player who helped develop these major league figures told me he thought they were much better role models than GI Joe and He-Man, and I agreed. Whatever the offenses of Boggs and his fellow athletes, few of them carry weapons and none aspires to master the universe.

I did get one piece of personal mail this week. It's a letter from an attorney in Chicago who says he thinks he remembers me as his summer school English teacher 20 years ago. The letter is complimentary, so it's a shame he's obviously got me confused with someone else. In order to have been teaching English in 1968, I'd have to be 40 years old now, and that can't be true. If I were 40, I'd certainly have at least ten or twelve years in the big leagues behind me, and I'm still waiting to be called up from the Cambridge Municipal Fastpitch League, C Division.

GOLF ON THE RUN

Golf's answer to Al Campanis, Hall W. Thompson, should have kept his mouth shut . . . or at least that's what country club golfing buddies from coast to coast are doubtless thinking these days. Challenged earlier this summer to explain why Shoal Creek, the Birmingham golf club he founded in 1977, had no black members, Mr. Thompson replied, "That's just not done in Birmingham." He has since claimed that he was quoted out of context, but an appropriate context for the remark is hard to imagine.

The membership policy of Mr. Thompson's club would merely be an ugly local story, except that Shoal Creek is scheduled as the site of the Professional Golfers' Association (PGA) Championship this summer. The Reverend Joseph Lowery, President of the Southern Christian Leadership Conference, has announced plans to picket the club, and several of the corporations which were supposed to sponsor the television coverage of the tournament have already bailed out, claiming that the climate at the PGA Championship is not "environmentally correct" for advertising, whatever that means . . . Maybe the place stinks.

The club's response has been interesting. Several members assured Birmingham's Mayor Richard Arrington that the club would accept black members within a year, and some have suggested that the Mayor himself — who is black — should be accepted as an honorary member right away as a gesture of good faith. That's a move that wouldn't be too threatening to the good ol' boys on the links. "Heck," they're probably saying to each other on the first tee even now, "he's practically one of us. He's a damn mayor!"

The imp of the perverse in me suggests that this situation out of the 60s should be handled otherwise. It calls for the loony, anarchic energy of Woodstock and beyond. Why doesn't ABC, the network which will cover the action from Shoal Creek, demand that the club immediately admit Tina Turner, B.B. King, and Little Richard, waving the $35,000 initiation fee for each?

I know racism is a serious issue, but this particular instance of it, this smug time capsule of ignorant elitism, calls for a really stupid and pointless gesture out of the days of Yippie Power and *revolution for the hell of it!* Why not throw the most foolish and grotesque prejudices of these Birmingham linksters in their faces? Why doesn't some helicopter pilot with an imagination fly over Shoal Creek and drop watermelon rinds all over the sacred greens? If Mayor Arrington is offered a membership in the club, I hope he'll at least bring a hellacious boom box into the locker room.

Shoal Creek is not, as they say, unrepresentative. *The Charlotte Observer* has found that 17 clubs that are sites of PGA tour events have all-white memberships. This is not surprising. Private golf clubs have long been the preserve of wealthy white men, who use these vast expanses as informal weekend boardrooms, where they plan the looting of Savings and Loan Associations and the devastation of the rain forests for monstrous profit. It's about time their black brothers and sisters got a chance to get their fingers in the pie.

I'm kidding, I'm kidding, I *swear* it!

The systematic exclusion of people because of race, creed, color, sex, etc., from *any* place is stupid, wrong, and shameful. The PGA and Shoal Creek and like institutions deserve all the picketing and abuse that outraged citizens of all colors can heap upon them.

But it's 1990, folks: over 40 years since Jackie Robinson broke the color line in big league baseball; nearly 30 years since the PGA of America extracted a "Caucasian only" clause from its own hallowed bylaws.

1990.

If you don't laugh a little, you're likely to cry.

"No Batta Batta Batta!"

I don't know what inning they were in when I arrived, and as long as I watched there was no sense of progress to the proceedings. Almost everybody on each team either walked or struck out.

All the focus was on the nine-year-old boy who was pitching. "Hang in there," somebody's father shouted at him. The pitcher sighed magnificently, fell half-heartedly into his motion, and threw a ball that bounced once in front of the batter, then skittered past the hot, exhausted catcher. Two base runners bestirred themselves and raced on to the next stations to wait again. Two of the outs that inning would come when kids tried to score from third on pitches like that. Both times they would slide so early that they would not reach home, and the catcher would have time enough to trap the ball as it bounced around in the backstop, hurry to the plate, and tag them out.

My favorite moment came when the coach of the team in the field called time-out and jogged to the mound to confer with his embattled hurler. The coach was young, bespectacled, athletic-looking. I couldn't hear what he was saying, but he began demonstrating in slow motion the act of pitching, over and over. After each sequence he would pause, as if to see if anyone had questions. After the third or fourth repetition, the pitcher piped, "I know how to do it!" and stomped his sneaker. The coach clapped the boy on the shoulder and jogged back to the bench. The next pitch sailed high over the catcher's lazily outstretched glove.

Or maybe that wasn't my favorite moment. The tableau of the left fielder chewing idly on the thumb of his mitt was good, too. Nobody was going to hit it *that* far, and he knew it, but until three guys on the other team swung wildly three times or haphazardly ran into outs, he was stuck there. Sometimes he looked longingly at the jungle gym and the swings on the other side of the playground, as if wondering whether anyone would notice if he ran over and played there for a while.

None of these kids was headed for the bigs, that was certain, though some of them might have had dreams.

Certainly a few had the tics and habits down. One second baseman had mastered the nonchalant little toe scratch in the dirt that professional middle infielders feature after they've handled the ball. Some of them chattered well . . . "Hummm, babe. No batta, batta, batta." This should not be underestimated. Shouting "You got this guy!" to a pitcher who has just walked six or eight hitters is an act of considerable imagination, a quality that must be encouraged in children.

After a while I turned from the game and walked back toward my car. Behind me I heard the scuttle and chirp of sides changing. The sun was a little lower in the blue evening sky. Soon one team would somehow win, and the other would lose. There would be cheers and ritual handshakes. Some players would toss their gloves into the air, and others would put theirs on their heads, dreamily trying to remember the score or forget it. And then everyone would go for ice cream.

STILL AIN'T GOT NO PEARL

I've been going to ball games since I was six, and I've never come home with a baseball.

Sometimes when I was a child, a foul fly would arc into the vicinity of my seat. But always some beefy adult would lean into the path of the ball and snatch it away, or else a fearless big kid would shoulder me aside in the scramble for the prize as it kicked around in the crowd.

Like a lot of children, I used to bring my glove to the game. But I never had the opportunity to use it. Actually, up to a point, this was probably a blessing. In my early baseball days — the days of the Cub Scout League — I was a third baseman. Then, one day some fellow eight-year-old lifted a pop-up toward me. "I got it! I got it!" I shouted with real (if ungrammatical) enthusiasm. I had my glove, of course. I probably got it up near the ball, too. But in the end it hit me square in the eye. Error, third base. (E-5, if you're keeping score at home.) Might have been the same story in the seats at the Polo Grounds.

Many years later I almost got a ball in the Fenway Park bleachers. It would have been a cheapie. Billy Martin, managing the Texas Rangers at the time, was shagging balls with his outfielders before the game. Occasionally he'd turn and toss one up into the crowd. The guy sitting next to me caught one. He was skinny and not especially athletic. I could have shouldered him out of the way, but I didn't think of it in time. Even in the bleachers it would have been unseemly to rip the ball out of his hands after he'd caught it.

Then, earlier this season, I got another chance. I'd flown down to Baltimore to see a game in Memorial Stadium, since the Orioles will abandon the park after this year. I was sitting in the sling, the tiny afterthought that hangs just below the press box and just above the protective screen behind home plate. You climb down a metal ladder to enter it. It's like getting into a submarine. Anyway, during an otherwise uneventful at-bat, Mo Vaughn, the large and menacing Red Sox rookie, nicked the bottom of a fastball and sent it rocketing back toward me.

In half a heartbeat, I learned that I am old and slow and cowardly. The inclination to try to catch the ball never glimmered along a single synapse. It was all *Dive! Dive!* I fell right, and my hat and sun glasses went left. The ball crashed into the wall behind me. My neighbor in the sling cautiously waited until it had stopped rolling, right at his feet. Then he picked it up.

"You know," he said as I groped around for my hat and glasses, feeling like Charlie Brown after one of those line drives back through the box has undressed him . . . "You know, I've been coming to the ballpark for years, and I've never gotten a ball before."

It's 36 years for me now and still counting. But at least my nose is still the shape genetics dictated, a trade-off I'm inclined to accept here in the middle innings.

ℝ

TIGER LOSES

They're cutting up the golf carts
    From Augusta to St. Paul
  And selling them for scrap
    To iron mongers . . . that's not all.

The fairways are tomato patches.
    Roughs have gone for hay.
  Latrobe out to LaCosta,
    This is golfing's darkest day.

The youngsters who'd begun the game
    Now hang out on the corner.
  Each caddie, lost and mumbling, looks
    Exactly like a mourner.

The clubs are losing members,
    And their parking lots are bare.
  In their silent dining rooms barkeeps
    Read, doze, or comb their hair.

What's happened to this once-hot game?
    What's turned its fortunes sour?
  What's crimped the hose of profit
    And made cheerful golfers dour?

What's rendered that green real estate,
    Where fell the bouncing ball,
  The future site of some developer's
    Grim shopping mall?

The answer? Tiger failed. He didn't win.
   He choked. He clutched.
 This boy-man among men,
    This paragon the gods had touched
 And lifted to the heights
    Of golfing greatness as a lad
 Became, in that last round of
    The Colonial, so bad
 That he hit a shot into the water,
    Took two double bogeys,
 And generally astonished
    Lots of ancient golfing fogeys
 Who turned, each to the other, and said,
    "Hey, we could do that!
 And we do. So what's the point?
    And each one turned just like the rat
 Who leaves the sinking ship and
    Scuttles off for higher land.
 And the myth of Tiger Woods fell
    Like a chip shot to the sand.

He lost. He finished fourth.
   His magic swing could not prevail.
 It was as if Excalibur had cracked:
    Beyond the pale . . .

And so the wind howls cold
   Across the empty golfing links,
 Where once the Tiger's legions roamed
    And bought each other drinks.

The putting greens are barren
   And the pro shops shuttered, too,
 And the lesson is that Tiger's human.
    I'll be darned! Who knew?

Can golf recover? Maybe.
   If so, where? And how? And when?
 It's simple. Soon as Tiger Woods
   Steps up and wins again.

FOOTBALL DREAMS

On hot days in the middle of summer, I sometimes think of how I once wanted to play football. It was odd that I should have had such an idea. It would have been in the days before television and the beer companies had wrapped the NFL in the flag, put its most elegantly gruesome movements to music, and elevated the dance to heroic proportions. So maybe it was just hormones.

Anyway, I was going to a new school. Nobody would know that I'd never played football. Maybe I could quietly learn the game. I was bigger than I'd been the year before, though still skinny. But I was tall. Maybe I'd be an end. Who knew? Maybe I'd make spectacular catches and tumble acrobatically over the goal line each Saturday while girls in tight sweaters with pom-poms danced and screamed for more.

Never mind that the school I was entering was all male. The dreams of adolescence easily leap limitation. Besides there would be faculty daughters, lithe and doe-eyed. And there was a girls' school down the street. It was 1963. What else would they have to do on a fall Saturday afternoon but watch the boys crash into one another? . . . Except for me, who would elude the crashing, gather in the desperate pass with educated fingers, seem to hang impossibly in the air for the photographers, then fall into the endzone and victory.

It was not, of course, that way.

On the first day of practice, we were issued all the equipment; the hip pads, shoulder pads and helmet that turn an 88-degree afternoon into a dangerous time to be meat. And then, in an exercise that had no place in my fantasies, one of the coaches lined a bunch of us up against each other and instructed both lines to block. What did I know about blocking or being blocked? I was destined to soar, not block. I might have tried to explain the coach's mistake to him, but from inside the helmet the words — muffled by a rubber mouthpiece — would only have buzzed and echoed without effect.

The whistle blew. Opposite me a boy who'd been listening more carefully — a boy undistracted by visions — lept across the line and charged up me as if I were a flight of stairs. He knew how to make an impression. His knee slammed into the front of my new helmet, and I toppled over like a tree.

I'm told I was only unconscious for a few seconds, but it was long enough for a clear thought to form itself, even in the overheated helmet. I opened my eyes and looked at the high blue sky and into the burning sun, and I said to myself, "Tennis. I'll play tennis."

⚑

LONG MAY HE BRING IT

A week ago, before 51,333 fans in Milwaukee and almost 8,000 big screen television viewers at Arlington Stadium in Texas, Nolan Ryan won the 300th game of his 22-year career. The twentieth pitcher in major league history to have reached that milestone, Nolan Ryan has simply done his job.

Half a dozen times he has done it spectacularly enough to record a no-hitter. Nobody has done that more often. But baseball history is less likely to remember him as *spectacular* than as *enduring*. So far, his career has lasted approximately 44 times as long as that of Deion Sanders.

At present, Ryan has the worst won-lost percentage of any pitcher to win 300 games. Through his first five seasons he was a losing pitcher. This is partly because he used to walk nearly everyone he didn't strike out, but mostly because he's played the better part of his career for teams that ranged from mediocre to wretched. This year, he's won more than twice as often as he's lost for another Texas *also ran*. In 1969, the only season during which he played for a world champion, Ryan pitched two-and-a-third innings of a World Series game. He walked 2, struck out 3, and was credited with a save, a marvelously ironic footnote to the career of a man who's won more games than all but 19 starting pitchers in the history of Major League Baseball.

There are other statistics, of course. In an excellent game in Boston earlier this season, Ryan became the only pitcher in big league history to strike out 100 or more hitters in 22 seasons. Wade Boggs, who has won five batting championships, struck out three times against Ryan that day. During her brief time in the spotlight last year, Margo Adams (Boggs's former girlfriend), revealed that Boggs had told her he regularly got so upset on the nights before he was going to hit against Ryan that he'd throw up. As far as I know, nobody has ranked pitchers on the number of batters whose stomachs they upset before games. But if there were such a category, Nolan Ryan would probably lead the league in it.

Actually, my favorite Ryan statistic is the number of his teammates who were under five years old — that is, too young to read about him — when he began his career: it stands at 19.

Beyond statistics, Nolan Ryan has stood for all sorts of admirable things. He has been unflappable in a sportsworld more and more given over to explosions of temper and fits of pique. He has been less inclined toward self-promotion than many, many players who have had much less to promote. He has credited his teammates, often more generously than they have deserved. He has appreciated the appreciation of his fans; after he won number 300 in Milwaukee, he apologized for the inconvenience to the folks from Texas who had to leave home to see the milestone victory.

None of this is to suggest that Nolan Ryan, winner of 300 games, pitcher of 6 no-hitters, fanner of batters nearly too numerous to count, is a hero in any cosmic sense. He is a workman who has been paid extremely well for his work; well enough, they say, to have recently bought a bank.

Now he's in the middle of this season of the sentencing of Pete Rose, reminding us of baseball's capacity to delight us with the story of a long career of quiet work. In this case, the career of a 43-year-old pitcher who still throws hard enough so that when most ballplayers are asked to explain how he does it, they can only shake their heads.

Nolan Ryan. Long may he bring it.

☞

STARTING EARLY

From my office window I can watch the tennis campers on their way to work. And it does look like work. On the court they practice running forwards and backwards, like football players. Then teen-aged instructors line them up and hit balls at their feet. Some of the tennis campers are only slightly taller than the racquets, of which some of them carry as many as four.

This is not *summer camp* as in: time to fool around in the lake, tip over a canoe for the fun of it, make a lanyard in the shade on a hot afternoon. There is no fooling around with archery here; no lying on a lumpy mattress with the worn stock of an old .22 against your cheek. Nope, this is serious; serious enough so that — on days when it rains and they can't play tennis — the campers are likely to meet with a sports psychologist who'll help them round their tennis attitudes into shape.

It's not just tennis, of course. There are hockey camps and football camps; baseball camps and soccer camps; even soccer *goalie* camps for children who have already specialized by the time they are old enough to sleep away from home.

This tendency to come early to full-time concentration on a sport is not new. Caroline Keggi, a second-year player on the Ladies Pro Golf Tour, said in a recent interview that at the age of 12 she was a good tennis player and a good golfer, but her tennis coach told her it was time to choose. At 12. And who could blame her coach? Perhaps he or she could see that in the next decade, the Jennifer Capriatis of the world would be turning pro at 14.

Old timers — particularly baseball old timers — complain that they never see kids just playing ball on their own anymore. It's a tired refrain, but it's true. With the exception of the playground basketball players, who will apparently always be with us, the kids are at camp sharpening their skills and their psyches. Last summer I even heard about a sportscasters' camp, where kids so young that they still should have been dreaming of becoming firemen could learn from the pros how to sit on their backsides and *describe* games with the mix of hysteria and polish that apparently takes years of practice to achieve.

I suppose in the spirit of all this I should open up a sports commentators' camp. I could take the campers on field trips to the baseball camps and the tennis camps and the soccer camps in the area, and they could interview the little boys and girls as they struggled to achieve excellence. Then they could put together packages of features and commentaries so I could critique them and send them out again to do better. There'd probably be money in that. We could have a t-shirt with the camp logo: I don't know, perhaps a baseball surrounded by microphones, or a microphone surrounded by baseballs.

I could do that.

Or I could make a call or two and see if I could find someone who wants to go over to the empty ballfield for a while and have a catch.

꒰

BASEBALL ON THE CLOCK

You like to think that as a species, we are moving in the right direction, getting wiser as we go along. And then out of the blue comes indisputable evidence that it's just not so.

A colleague of mine recently took in a baseball game — or part of one — for the first time in years, and as soon as he got home, he sat down and banged out the following suggestions for improving the game, then sent them to me. *Rules Changes to Speed Up Baseball*, he called them:

1. No team may use more than two pitchers per game.
2. If a pitcher cannot pick-off a baserunner in three attempts, the runner may advance to the next base.
3. A pitcher may not tug at the brim of his cap more than two times per batter.

Actually this is only a sample of the *nine* suggestions my colleague had . . . nice symmetry in that number, and I suppose I should be grateful that he didn't suggest cutting games to three innings, or innings to two outs.

In fairness, I'll acknowledge that there are a few painless ways to cut excessively long baseball games. For one thing, you could exterminate the mascots that are always flopping up to managers and swatting umpires. For another, you could shave the TV time out between innings with no damage to the quality of the game. And then you could knock off replays on the huge TV screens most parks now have. If people aren't paying attention, that's *their* bad judgment. But these are matters tangential to the game itself, and people like my colleague are less interested in them than in diminishing baseball without any sensitivity.

Anyway, I wrote back to him right away. "I understand your dismay," I said, "but why limit your suggestions for speeding up things to baseball?" Here are some others to consider:

1. So-called *gourmet meals* take an awfully long time, don't they? It seems to me restaurants should be limited to serving two courses, tops; if they insisted on serving more, they'd have to serve them all at once, on the same plate.
2. What about this preposterous notion that wine should be allowed to age, to develop character over months or years? Seems to me faster wine would be better wine. Maybe there ought to be a rule that vintners would have, oh, six days, max, to get their product from the vine to the packy.
3. Then there's literature. Boy, have I had it with those laggards who say it sometimes takes years to write a good novel. Sounds like self-indulgent rubbish to me. Publishers ought to put stopwatches on those clowns and let 'em know that they'll only be paid while they're turning out the stuff at, say, 35 words a minute. Along the same line, it's silly to have to wade through long books like *War and Peace* or *Finnegan's Wake*. Maybe we should just limit books to 100 pages or less. And while we're at it, we could cut all art down to wallet size and forget this pretentious museum and gallery business.

I had other suggestions, too: about limiting vacations to weekends and relationships to one-night stands, but I didn't want to run on. I figured I'd be defeating my own purpose if I wrote this guy a *long* letter.

⚑

COLORS

Here's the sort of off-season football news I like, because it has nothing to do with drugs, felonious assault, drunken driving, surgery, or anybody getting fired. The Atlanta Falcons, 25 years old next season, are apparently thinking about going to all black uniforms.

My mother was visiting when I read that news.

"They'll look like a ballet troupe," she said.

But I'm not sure. Maybe the Falcons will look fearsome. Black and silver have served the Raiders well, encouraging an outcast bad guy mentality among members of that team. All black might work even better, especially if the Falcons go with black numbers, too, because then they'd be not only outcast and bad, but also mysterious, like Darth Vadar.

This will only seem like a trivial issue to someone who's never played an organized sport. Anyone who's worn an athletic uniform knows how important the details of such a uniform are. I still remember the first basketball uniform I got to wear as a third-grader in the Cub Scout League. It included those shiny, satiny pearl white shorts with a blue stripe. Exceedingly spiffy, at least in my nine-year-old estimation of things.

The Little League in the town where I grew up had a cruel policy regarding uniforms. The kids who made the regular teams got uniforms modeled on the big league clubs from which they took their names. As a Commonwealth Cardinal, I wore a facsimile of the splendid jersey the St. Louis Cardinals wear: white with *Cardinals* across the front; a bat and the red bird itself featured prominently in the design. The uniform shirts and pants were made of a flannel that got hot and sticky, just like what the pros wore then. And we got genuine wool baseball caps, too. Uncomfortable as could be, but genuine.

Meanwhile the kids who didn't make the big clubs and had to play tee-ball down at the minor league park got only crumby cotton t-shirts and mesh caps with no logo at all. No wonder most of them quit after a week or so. All they had to do was look in the mirror to see that *they* weren't ballplayers.

My favorite uniform when I got to college was the hockey uniform I wore as an intramural player. We had the jerseys the intramural football team had discarded. Faded yellow with black they were. Mine was faded nearly to white, in fact, and the stitching on the numbers let go a little more each game, so the digits sort of flapped against my back when I stopped hard. I wore number 87, a claim which not many hockey players can make.

Across the spectrum of sports, certain uniforms bespeak class. Traditional Yankee pinstripes, for example, retain their elegance despite the bozo who owns the team. The San Diego Padres, on the other hand, will look like clowns if the franchise lasts a hundred years.

It's perhaps a measure of the decline of my own prospects as a ballplayer that for the last dozen years I've played for a team the members of which — for the most part — refuse to have anything to do with uniforms, although a lot of the other teams in the league spend hundreds of dollars outfitting themselves. My teammates generally wear an assortment of caps and shirts and sweatpants that look as if they came from different bins in the same baseball thrift shop, except when our team captain is running for office. Twice over the last eight years he's sold us all t-shirts that promoted his candidacy for District Attorney, and for a while we've actually looked like a team until the shirts have worn out. There is a rumor afoot now that the captain has become restless in his job . . . that he's ready to scale greater heights. If this is so, we'll all wear new shirts proclaiming our support for our man's run at the Attorney General's office.

We'll look like a team once again, and there'll be some of the Little Leaguer's pleasure in the game, for those of us inclined to admit it.

ß

A CURRENT AFFAIR

I'm here to remind you of river swimming.

Swimming in a pool is fine, I suppose, but there is almost necessarily too much of the serious in it. Swimming in a pool is laps. Swimming in a pool is toddlers rousted out of bed at dawn, driven in carpools to the country club, then brow-beaten by some witless perfectionist of a coach about pain and gain. Swimming in a pool is burned-out, red-eyed, 15-year-olds who'd just as soon leave laps to their younger brothers and sisters.

Swimming in a pool is Mark Spitz, laboring — probably, even as I speak — against a stopwatch that doesn't care. Maybe you think Mark Spitz's attempt to swim in the Olympics again is brave, a stirring effort to demonstrate that you're never too old to excel. Maybe you think Spitz is simply a pathetic case of arrested development, a grown-up without imagination enough to find something better to do with his life than swim laps. Whatever. The laps he is swimming now, and the thousands more that he will swim are work. *Slap, slap,* touch, turn, kick, *slap, slap,* work.

Ocean swimming is work of another kind. Ocean swimming is a macho exercise. In the ocean, you cut through the waves, take breakers on your chest, and risk a wipeout and a mouth full of sand every time you go in deep enough to get your bathing suit wet. Ocean swimming is the sign that says *No Lifeguard on Duty*. The unstated subtext is: *Take your chances, Bub, but don't blame us if you end up headed for Japan while the seagulls mock your progress.*

Ocean swimming is endurance. Ocean swimmers start in England, rub grease all over their bodies, and end up in France, unless they have to be pulled — exhausted and hallucinating — into boats, in which case they weep in humilation and swear they'll try again as soon as they can stop shaking.

Some people like to swim in lakes, but I've never understood it. Lakes are, by definition, bodies of water that are dying. They are usually surrounded by picnic tables, at which huge, holiday crowds of huge people fight each other over potato chips and the last beer. Their children shriek when their wobbling Frisbees veer into the lake by mistake. This is high drama on a lake. It has always seemed to me that while the fish in the ocean are likely to be hostile and the fish in a river are likely to be energetic, playful, and clever, the fish in a lake are probably as dumb as they look. The fish in a pool are made out of plastic.

River swimming is discovering the rhythm and ride of the river and giving yourself up to it and finding that it's perfectly happy to show you the way. The river I visited recently had a number of great places to swim. My favorite was a spot where two streams came together and created a playful current which carried south for a while and then dumped you into a little eddy, where a second current would gently return you to the rock you'd slid off to begin with.

I watched a couple of 10- and 12-year-olds play this game first. One was a girl who was pretty tentative about the whole thing, but she eventually decided to give it a try. She slipped off the flat rock, and the river caught her and bobbed her down stream, where I heard this terrific involuntary giggle. In the ocean, you hear the scream of surprise. In the lake, you hear the sigh of stupor. In the pool, you hear the gasp of lungs overworked. Give me the involuntary giggle every time.

When it was my turn, the river carried me along, too. It didn't care that I weigh more than I did in college. I was as easy on the river as the slender 10-year-old had been.

I offer all this as a public service, I guess. It's only the middle of July. The rivers are out there.

ぞ

FROM THE END OF THE BENCH

I play on an old fast pitch softball team.

By *old*, I don't just mean that the team has been around for a long time, although it has. I mean that in a league composed mostly of students, recent graduates or dropouts, the team I play for has a lot of old guys. Our best pitcher is far enough along so that his 19-year-old son starts for us in left field. And he's not entirely unrepresentative.

In fact, that left fielder is part of a gradual youth movement we've experienced on the club over the past couple of years. Guys in their 20s have come along to play some of the so-called *skill* positions: shortstop and catcher, for example. At shortstop, range is an issue, and old legs lack range; at catcher, some of us who've filled in behind the plate on short-handed nights haven't been able to walk normally for several days thereafter.

Anyhow, the gradual youth movement has allowed us to play with a minimum amount of embarrassment a first baseman and a designated hitter who have about 40 years of combined baseball experience.

And I, for one, have adjusted pretty well to the changes. It hasn't bothered me to watch younger guys glide over in front of ground balls that I could only have waved at, or snap off throws that would have left me reaching for ice or Bengay.

It's been sort of fun to see a couple of fellas play who could bunt for a base hit. There were years when that thought never crossed the mind of anybody in the lineup; years when I'm not sure we even had a bunt sign. The return of the bunt has been very enjoyable.

But something happened at a practice recently that left me wondering whether I was still playing the same game as these youth movement members of the team. We were taking batting practice — just batting practice, nothing to get excited about or strain yourself over — and somebody hit a foul ball over the chainlink fence down the left field line. I'd started loping down along the fence toward the gate to get the ball out of the street, when, suddenly, one of the youth movement guys — I think he was playing shortstop — started racing *full speed* at the fence. In one motion he dropped his glove, took the top of the fence in his hands, and vaulted over it . . . *effortlessly.* Then he picked up the ball, tossed it back to the batting practice pitcher, and vaulted the fence again, this time without even a running start.

I've been thinking about it since, and I've decided that I can remember the last time I reached the catcher in the air with a throw from the outfield. And I can remember the last time I played shortstop — in another league altogether — and took a groundball bare-handed, then threw out the runner at first.

But I can't remember the last time I vaulted a chainlink fence. I can't remember that. And I wish I'd been cleaning my spikes, or looking the other way when that kid did it.

⚑

In August They're In Saratoga

To do it right, you have to get up early.

It's August, and the fastest thoroughbred horses in the world are running at the historic track in Saratoga Springs, New York. Post time for the first race is 1PM, but for the insiders — the people who train and exercise these million dollar horses — the day begins much earlier.

At the Whitney Training Track — a one-mile oval surrounded on two sides by pastures and trees, and on a third by the impossibly neat wooden shed row that's housed 46 horses for the past five weeks — Bill Mott supervises the thoroughbreds he's training for himself and a number of other owners. Mott, the most successful trainer during the present meet, is a hands-on guy. At dawn, he rides alongside Cigar, a candidate for Horse of the Year. A North Dakota boy whose father was a veterinarian, Mott started training horses as a teenager 30 years ago. He is a man supremely well-fitted for his work, though he doesn't see it precisely that way.

"Number one," he told me, "I'm probably not capable of doing much else. I think my talents are very limited. I think I'd better try to do the best I can at this and keep it going for as long as I can, because there's not much else that I know about."

By 6:45, when the sun makes it over the trees to the east

of the training track and turns the soft dirt on the far side of the oval from dark to caramel brown, Mott and his staff have already worked out the first set of seven horses. Four hours later, exercise rider Louise Teeter Bray finally has the opportunity to talk about how she came to horse racing, a process apparently as inevitable for her as it was for her boss.

"Well," she says with a shrug, "I don't think I had a shot. I've always been in love with horses. My grandfather was a trainer. My father was a breeder and raced horses, so I was around them all my life. I was in college studying animal science, and I had a kind of a rough semester, and I had the job working with the thoroughbreds. I was gonna take one semester off, and it just —"

She can't finish the sentence for the giggle. She never went back to school.

"Is it a good life?" I ask her. "Is it good work?"

"It can be very gratifying and fulfilling. When you're on a horse, and you can accomplish what you're supposed to accomplish with that horse, it's very gratifying. But, ah, the money's not all that great, and if you do this for a living, you do it because you love it."

The Whitney Track isn't open to the public, of course, but that doesn't mean there's nowhere for the seeker of the track's truth and beauty to go before the racing starts. At about 7AM, the patio adjoining the clubhouse at Saratoga opens for breakfast. The strawberries and French toast are only part of the attraction. While you eat, you can listen as Mary Ryan identifies the horses, the jockeys, and the trainers over the clack and rattle of the cups and silver.

As jockey Eddie Maple works a horse along the rail opposite Ryan's stand, she says into her microphone, "Eddie Maple in the red sweatshirt, and going the wrong way . . . Eddie Maple and I have been around for a long time, and when I say that, he always says to me, 'Mary, do you have to tell them that?'"

Eddie Maple, standing in the irons, waves and smiles.

"Preparation for this job started 25 years ago," Mary Ryan tells me. "The background knowledge. And then, of course, for current news I have to keep reading the racing form, the post parade, the trade magazines, and watch the races."

Over the years, I've seen patrons approach Mary for tips on the races. Why not? Who knows more about what these horses can do? I wonder out loud if she helps anyone out.

"Oh, Bill, I get that question a lot of times," she says. "You know what I tell everyone who asks for a hot horse? I say the winner of the race will be the first horse across the finish line . . . officially."

If that's not the sort of humor you appreciate, you can finish your coffee, smile at the women modeling the latest summer frocks, and walk across the road. There each morning a professional handicapper will share his wisdom for free with anyone who can squeeze into the tent beside Ciro's Restaurant. Some of those gathered for tips feverishly write down everything the expert says. Others don't. One middle-aged New Yorker cheerfully admitted to me that he bets birthdays, house numbers, and his kids' ages. His friend laughed and said, "Yeah, and then you turn the numbers around if you feel like it, and then you look at the board and throw it all out and bet on whatever horse seems right."

"That's it," the first man agreed. "Then when the race is over, we look at each other and say, 'Now why did we bet that horse?'"

When the track finally opens for business and the crowd arrives, the people-watching begins. The young and the restless are here, and the old and the lonely. The imperially slim owners, the loud, cigar-chomping railbirds, and the stoopers, who will spend the brilliant afternoon bending over, examining the pavement and the grass for winning tickets discarded by mistake. There are celebrities, too, and near-celebrities, and they all have some connection to this glorious race track. One morning, with an assist from the superbly well-connected Mary Ryan, I met Ben Cohen, the co-founder of Ben and Jerry's Ice Cream.

"I started coming to the race track when I was a Pinkerton Guard," he said with a smile. "I was on the midnight to eight shift. My job was to guard the Travers Canoe that's behind the tote board. College kids used to like to steal it. They gave me a whistle. If somebody tried to steal the canoe, I was supposed to whistle. I can proudly report that nobody stole it on my watch."

I don't know how well Ben Cohen made out at the track that day. I can report that I found a winner in the first race, a steeple chase, with a foolproof system: I bet the female jockey. The second race should have been easy. Bill Mott, the trainer I'd met earlier and whom everyone had been celebrating, was entering a horse named Exotica. On paper he was six lengths better than anything else in the gate. But Exotica threw his jockey before the start, ran halfway around the track, wore himself out, and got scratched from the race.

Even when your inside information and your hunch coincide under a perfect sky at the world's prettiest track, things aren't simple at the races. But the inscrutability and even the potential for mayhem, unseated riders, and bolting horses are part of the charm, and there is no track anywhere more charming. Over the years, the meet at Saratoga, which used to run only during August, has been extended to five and then six weeks. Still, it is shorter and more precious than any meet at Aqueduct or Belmont, and even the Saratoga townies, who watch their burg turn into a great big festival of racing and betting each summer, miss it when the horses and owners and trainers and patrons depart.

"It's a mixture of relief and sadness," Karen Schwartz, a graphic designer in Saratoga told me. "But it's mostly sadness. When the track closes, it's definitely fall here."

꒛

LOSING BASEBALL

At the height of the Red Sox rush, when they could not lose a game, I talked with 70-odd-year-old Johnny Pesky in the dugout at Fenway Park. When our conversation was over, I thanked him for his time.

"Sure," he said. "My pleasure."

Then his face crinkled into a smile, and he said, "I hope we keep winning." He might have been a child.

On one of the summer's hottest weekends, I drove to Falmouth and saw Bill Lee and his band of middle-aged teammates outfox and outhit the Commodores, a Cape Cod League team made up of gifted and powerful boys, some of whom will make the bigs and still be there when Lee is 60.

On another hot night, I followed several tortured sets of directions to one neighborhood field after another in search of a particular Thomas Yawkey League team I wanted to see. I found the team and watched a guy who'd once been a prospect, but hadn't pitched in six years. He got his club into extra innings and almost won.

And I played another year in the fast-pitch league in Cambridge . . . struck out on three pitches in the only at-bat my daughters saw and on another night banged a double over the head of an astonished left-fielder who *knew* I couldn't hit it *that* far.

And finally to the point: at that same dusty, badly-lighted field where I struck out and (weeks later) stroked the double — a field bounded by an elementary school and a busy Cambridge street — I lost baseball entirely for a while.

We were playing the late game, and by the middle innings it was fully dark. While I was waiting to either hit or return to my position at second base, I gradually became aware of the soft sound of singing. Down the street, through the trees and the wire fence, I could see the beginning of a procession of some kind.

A few minutes later, the marchers filled the street. They were women of all ages. They carried candles. They sang in Portuguese, and I couldn't understand the words (though sometimes I thought I could).

Someone said it was a holiday. It was eerie and beautiful, otherwordly, like something set in the middle of Mexico or somewhere else where visions aren't surprising and everyone joins in. But it was right there in front of a rock-strewn Cambridge ballyard.

I watched until the inning ended. Somebody had to tell me that the third out had occured. I took one last look at the procession disappearing down the street, behind the brick school, and I thought, "Maybe I won't go out to second base. Maybe I'll just follow them."

I remember the glowing candles and the serene faces of the singing women. I remember the soft surprise of their presence on that summer night. And I'm damned if I remember whether we won the game.

↱

LIKE FATHER, LIKE . . .

At the top of the line, you have Ken Griffey and his son in the big leagues at the same time. Then there's Carlton Fisk lifting weights with his son, the first baseman. From the coach's box in Baltimore, Cal Ripkin watches two of his sons play the infield.

Willie Mays is said to have started toddling after a slow grounder at six months. It was his father, an athlete so quick he was nicknamed *Kitty Cat*, who rolled the ball.

I never made it beyond the sandlots, and I have daughters. Still . . .

My older daughter is three-and-a-half now. When pressed, she will humor me for a few minutes by playing catch with a beanbag, but what she really wants to do is peel the thing open to see the beans. Last year sometime, a toy company sent me a little plastic Wade Boggs doll, which I gave to Amy. She played with it for a while, moving its arms to simulate swinging at a baseball, but mostly she lectured it for not going to bed on time.

"Wade Boggs," she'd tell it, "you behave yourself or you can't watch *Sesame Street* for a week."

Otherwise, baseball's charms are limited as far as Amy is concerned, though the game does show up in one peculiar ritual every now and then. Before her bath, sometimes, she wraps herself in the shower curtain and says, "You can't come in my baseball game," . . . a spooky and precise commentary on my availability when the Red Sox are on TV, I'm afraid.

My younger daughter is just over four months old, and for her I have higher hopes. When I hand her a baseball, she grasps it happily. Sometimes she tumbles over, as if making a spectacular catch. She will examine the ball for as long as two or three seconds before trying to cram it into her mouth. The other day, just for the hell of it, I called her *Lefty*, and she smiled and giggled. She also smiles and giggles at the toaster oven, but still . . .

I know I must be prepared for more difficult times. My brother-in-law, who played minor league ball for a year, tried to encourage in his toddler son an interest in the game. There is a picture of him doing this: holding out a baseball to the little boy, who is impishly walking in the other direction.

And then there is my neighbor, the former soccer coach. He enrolled his four-year-old daughter in a youth soccer program and then watched, appalled, from the sideline as she stood stock still while all the other youngsters happily chased the ball up and down the field. Once one of the coaches went over to speak to the stationary child, and when the game was over, my neighbor asked his daughter what instructions she'd received. She smiled at him and said, "The coach told me that if I stayed in one place long enough, I'd grow roots. Isn't that funny?" He didn't think so.

Like me, this neighbor has two daughters. Like me, he hopes that they will eventually come to find in sports the same fun and satisfaction which we have found. To that end, we took the two older girls down to the Boston Common one afternoon late last summer, when a very good high school softball pitcher named Lisa Moore was going against Eddie Fainer — The King and his Court — in a charity game. The girls watched quietly. Lisa Moore was brilliant. After a couple of innings, we walked over to the nearby public garden and took the kids for a ride on a swanboat.

When we got home, Amy rushed in to tell her mother about the day. "We went on the swanboat and saw the ducklings," she said happily.

"Great," my wife said. "What else did you do?"

My daughter thought about it for a moment, then said, "Well, we stood around and waited in the sun until it was *time* to go on the swanboat."

Maybe this year.

↳

BILLIE JEAN KING

In a frivolous moment during an autobiography she co-wrote a generation ago, Billie Jean King quipped: "At my funeral, nobody's going to talk about me. They're all just going to stand up and tell each other where they were on the night I beat Bobby Riggs."

A decade later, she wrote another autobiography. In this one she worried that folks would only remember her as the victim of a palimony suit brought by her former secretary and lover.

History will be kinder and fairer than that, or at least it should be. Assuming Billie Jean King ever slows down enough to become fodder for history, she will be remembered for playing 265 matches at Wimbledon, 40 more than her nearest competitor, counting singles, women's doubles, and mixed doubles. King won 20 Wimbledon titles, also a record. In a sport where burnout at 16 is not uncommon and Jimmy Connors is considered super-human for playing into his 30s, Billie Jean King was competitive in four different decades.

And in her case, *competitive* was most of the story. *Gifted*, *talented*, terms like that didn't really apply. She wasn't even the right *shape* for tennis. Female tennis players had previously been elegant rather than ornery and quiet rather than contentious, but King churned around the court like a little truck, loudly exhorting herself to greater concentration. "Come on, you idiot!" she'd shout at herself whenever she missed a volley. Her opponent would look to the referee for help, but in those days the referees could only shrug. Which of them had ever seen anyone like the goggle-eyed, battling King? Who knew what to make of her?

She should never have won at Wimbledon at all. The climate aggravated her asthma and allergies and she always played sick there. But it was her showplace for years. For her first singles win she got a plate and the six Mars bars some of her friends had left on her bed back at the hotel. A few years later, she became the first woman to make $100,000 a year at the game.

Nobody is likely to break Billie Jean King's Wimbledon record . . . unless it is Martina Navratilova, who has rung-up 17 titles there to date and just won the warm-up tournament. Ironically, if Navratilova does compete long enough to surpass King, King will be partly responsible. Earlier this year, Navratilova sought out King as a coach, and King has done her job so effectively that Navratilova has an excellent chance against the collected children of the draw. Nobody will be rooting harder for her than King, the pioneer to whom the Sabatinis and Capriotis of the tour owe a debt as large as the gulf between the Mars bars of yesterday and the millions of today.

℞

JUST DREAM ON

It's been a summer of ironies, great and small.

In the very first season in which the Boston Red Sox could finish first in their division — and even by doing so not necessarily prevent the New York Yankees from winning the World Series — our Sox have finished first.

The season began late because of the longest strike in the history of professional sports, and the opening "Play ball" rang hollow in a lot of half-empty ballparks. In New York, the fans who did show up threw dollar bills at the Mets. The fans who showed up in Pittsburgh threw flags wrapped in metal tubes at the Pirates. There was ugliness elsewhere, too, but not at Fenway Park.

Some Boston fans may have intended to show those dumb ol' greedy owners and dumb young greedy players, but when the bell rang, they couldn't help themselves. They found this team so darn likable. When the Sox threw a fan appreciation day, the faithful lined up around the block in the rain for autographs and a word or a smile from Jose Canseco, Mike Greenwell, and Tim Naehring. All was either forgiven by the compassionate, or forgotten by the unconscious; take your pick.

Either way, the outcome was the same: a season that has seen attendance figures dip elsewhere — no matter how well the home team has done — has been full of happy days at Fenway Park.

If the song for the overachieving '67 Red Sox was "The Impossible Dream" and the anthem of the '86 club was, inescapably, "McNamara's Band," then the theme this time around has got to be "You Made Me Love You (I Didn't Want to Do It)." The arrangement would be heavy on the strings.

There is irony, too, in the way these Red Sox have discovered first place and then camped there for the duration. This team has managed for the most part without longtime Big Guy Roger Clemens, counting instead on two newcomers. Tim Wakefield has pushed his silly Fluffernutter of a pitch past almost everybody, logging more innings than anyone but Erik Hanson. Hanson's the guy who has pitched better this season than in any since 1990, and who — as recently as 1992 — led the American League in losses. Both are here because Dan Duquette, the Sox' general manager, found them on someone else's discard pile and understood immediately that even if their signings were mistakes, they'd be cheap mistakes. Smart guy.

Duquette also deserves credit for acquiring various other worthies, including the exceptionally useful Willie McGee. Several years ago, given the opportunity to snap up a younger and, hence, even more useful version of the same McGee, Duquette's predecessor, Lou Gorman, went all wide-eyed, spread his arms, and asked rhetotically, "Where would we put him?" It's nice to see that question answered. (In the middle of a lineup that's gone and won a division title, Lou.)

Now, the happy echoes of the Night of the Clinching have faded, of course, and as the Sox play out the deliciously meaningless string, fans can turn and tack their dreams to a new, jumbo edition of the play-offs. Most of them, no doubt, are hoping the Red Sox will win the World Series. Where would they be if they couldn't count on us to so hope? But in that context, I have a confession to make.

In October 1986, back when Boston almost did win the World Series, I had contracted to write a story about the struggle, no matter who came out on top. When the Sox went up 3 games to 2 and I was walking out to Kenmore Square with several thousand elated people who wanted to see their team go down to New York and win that one more game, I suddenly realized that I wasn't sure I wanted it to happen.

I'd lived in Boston for 14 years. I should have been rooting for the Red Sox. But I was rooting for the story instead. If they won, it would be only another tale about another team that had lost for a long time and then had won. But if they lost — and what perverse way might they find to do it? — the story would be open-ended, still potentially infinite in its possibilities, and up to me.

It has been suggested that all bad marriages are the same, but that each good marriage is unique. With baseball teams, it's the other way around. All teams that win combine reasonably sound pitching, hitting and defense to do so. But teams that lose — especially teams that lose when everybody is watching — often find marvelously grotesque and inventive ways to fulfill what is apparently their destiny. And what stories we have when it happens again and again.

I've lived here for 23 years now. Certainly a part of me hopes this edition of the home team — this mercurial club, the roster of which has been changing in a blur as we've watched — will somehow prevail. But I cannot quite believe it will happen. I can't.

And the other part of me — the part that hopes it won't — perhaps feels that way because it's flat out spooky imagining a morning without the story I've been reading and writing and taking for granted for so long.

ꝑ

MICKEY MANTLE

It has been said of several habitually snarly ballplayers who've suddenly become approachable and garrulous as their careers have begun to evaporate that, "He's learning to say *hello*; now it's almost time to say *goodbye*."

Though the saying wouldn't have fit Mickey Mantle, the ballplayer, it has some resonance for Mickey Mantle, the man. At the end of his life, Mickey Mantle looked back at the waste — his own judgment of what he'd made of his extraordinary talent and his popularity — and he urged others to avoid his mistakes: specifically, the destructive drinking and the neglect of his family. Given a little more time to live by virtue of a liver transplant, he encouraged organ donation and established a foundation to continue that work after his death.

This was Mickey Mantle's second legacy. The first was the memory of his speed, his power, and the great joy with which he played baseball. If he spoke to our consciences at the end with the authority of a penitent, he spoke to our hearts 40 years ago and lifted them as the best athletes do with the grace of their best days. He wouldn't have said that was what he was doing — maybe he *couldn't* have said it — but that makes no difference. His triumphs were fun. They were public, and they were ours, no matter what Mickey Mantle did after work.

Which brings us to the business of what we've lost, now that Mickey Mantle is dead. It's no surprise that the pictures in the newspapers and magazines have given us this week are pictures of Mantle in his prime: pictures of his long and mighty swing, arms extended, neck muscles bulging; pictures of his diving catches and slides; pictures of his open, smiling face under a Yankee cap in the sunshine of the stadium. Mickey Mantle was 63 when he died, and the disease that killed him first exhausted and wasted him. But the pictures in the papers and the magazines of the youngster who couldn't have imagined ever growing old are the right pictures.

Nine years ago, when my father died, a colleague said to me, "The hard part about a father's death is that you lose your Daddy: not only the man who is old, but the man who was young and strong for you when you were a child."

When an athlete like Mickey Mantle dies — an athlete who was such a glowing and obviously gifted presence for the wide-eyed among us who watched him and watched Willie Mays and the rest when we were children and then teenagers and then adults — when an athlete like that dies, we lose the man, of course, but we also lose the boy. And some more of the boy in us.

ᛈ

SOX BACK

You're casting about for how to feel
  About this resurrection.
    Well, here's a word of caution . . . *listen*
    For your own protection.
    Don't climb aboard that wagon yet —
    The one beneath the band —
    You can't have lived here very long
    If you don't understand
    The way the Sox sneak up on you
    And grab your heart and yank
    And tug and make you think this time
    They won't dive in the tank.
    They plot this in the dugout,
    Between innings on the bench . . .
    "How can we suck them in this year?"
    They ask. "How can we wrench
    Their hearts out of their chests and leave
    Them weeping, cursing, swearing
    That *this* time we have driven them
    Beyond the point of caring?"

And this year? Why, they started off
  By losing everyday . . .

By kicking groundballs, dropping flies,
And pitching as if they
Were batting practice guys for all
The league's opposing hitters.
And they provoked our scorn and our
Derision and our titters.
And we said, "This is simple.
They are horrible, I think . . .
No need to watch the Sox at all
This year, because they stink!"
And each night in the clubhouse,
When the writers had retired,
The players and the manager
Sat down and they conspired
To play us all like violins
When they would begin winning;
And that is why, as fans, we are
More sinned against than sinning.

So, now they're back, or so they'd have you think,
And they're contending . . .
But that's just baseball's word for what
Precedes 'round here: the rending
Of garments and the piling on
Of sackcloth and of ashes,
For '96 must take its place
Beside the other crashes . . .
Unless, of course, it doesn't,
And the Sox go all the way
And win not just the wild card,
But the pennant, and then play
So well right through October,
Led by Wakefield, Vaughn, and Clemens
That this time everything comes up
Sweet roses and not lemons . . .
And Boston will be the champion,

129

And light will conquer dark,
And they'll never tear down Fenway
To create a bigger park.
And orphans will get in for nothing.
Hot dogs will be free!
And baseball will return to being
A game again, and we
Will all be young forever . . . that's the
Sort of freight we've heaped
Upon the Sox each season, and
The harvest that we've reaped
Is the consequence of caring and that
Feeble light ahead?
That's the hope we'll all pursue like
Idiots until we're dead.

BOXING:
WHY WE CAN'T QUITE LOOK AWAY
[AN ESSAY ACCOMPANYING AN EXHIBITION OF BOXING-RELATED ART]

"After the first punch is thrown, the fear is gone.
Then it's a form of joy."

Floyd Salas, Featherweight

Maybe you are one of those folks who screams for blood from a ringside seat, and more. In an essay on boxing, Joyce Carol Oates recalls a story Dustin Hoffman tells of an *ecstatic* boxing fan who followed the winner of a fight back to his dressing room, smearing himself with the sweat of the victorious boxer's body as he went. Maybe you are that sort of fight fan.

But if you are not, then there is probably tension at the center of your relationship to boxing. If you are alone with the TV set, clicking from channel to channel, and you find two men banging on each other, you probably watch for some moments, even if you hate what you are seeing. Perhaps no sport has the power of boxing to fascinate us and repel us at the same time, which is, of course, where the tension comes from. Intelligent, sensitive, sincere observers have compared boxing to chess and making love. Of course, it has also been compared, just as legitimately, to murder. And if boxing has undeniably been the route out of the ghetto, as the cliché has it, for some, it has also been the road to kidney damage, blindness, brain damage, and death for many, many others. So, tension.

And here is another punch and counter-punch. Boxing, certainly the least intrinsically funny sport our species has devised, has inspired funnier stories than any game but baseball. Here's proof.

At one point in his career when Muhammad Ali was squaring off against a succession of second-rate opponents, his handlers lined up a palooka named Chuck Wepner. For those not in the boxing know, Wepner was the battling unfortunate upon whose career Sylvester Stallone's *Rocky* was based. He was a *ham and eggs* fighter who'd never made enough in the ring to even afford a place where he could properly train. He made his living selling liquor in Bayonne, New Jersey. His face was so easily cut that he was nicknamed the *Bayonne Bleeder*. As a condition for signing for the fight against Ali, Wepner asked for an advance against his part of the gate, so he could leave his job for a few weeks and actually prepare for the bout. He got the money and worked himself into good enough shape so that he could delude himself into thinking he had a shot against the fastest, most exciting heavyweight in history. In fact, on the day of the fight, Wepner was so sure he would win that he bought his wife a sexy new negligée and told her, "Honey, I want you to wear this tonight, because you're gonna be sleeping with the heavyweight champion of the world."

The fight itself went about as everybody but Wepner thought it would go. By the time the referee stopped it, *the Bayonne Bleeder* was cut over both eyes, and his nose was badly broken. He could barely leave the ring under his own power. When he returned to his hotel room with 23 new stitches in his face, his wife, a vision in the negligee, was waiting for him. According to Wepner himself she took one look at him, waited a beat, and then said, "Okay, bigshot. Do I go to the champ's room, or does he come here?"

Of course, not all the stories are so funny. The story of how Korean boxer Deuk Koo Kim was beaten to death over 13 rounds by Ray Mancini isn't funny, nor is the tale of how Emile Griffith's barrage of punches kept the unconscious Benny Paret upright against the ring post, an attack so savage that even the referee was paralyzed by its fury. Norman Mailer has written of that fight that Paret was dead before he could fall down and that "Griffith's punches echoed in the mind like a heavy ax in the distance chopping into a wet log."

Mailer, Oates, A. J. Liebling, and any number of other wonderful writers have been drawn to boxing by the drama of it, which is both simple and complex. A punch, hard and fast enough to stun the brain, is simple enough, but a fighter can also win by pecking away at an opponent until he is confused, popping and nudging him from a dozen different directions, staying a half-second out of his way, until the opponent's understanding of time and space is temporarily scrambled. Ali was the master of that. He beat George Foreman by lying on the ropes, apparently so defenseless that even his corner man, the wily Angelo Dundee, confessed he had no idea what the champ was doing. Then, when the younger, stronger, but less imaginative Foreman had punched himself out, Ali stepped away from the ropes and put his man down without a wasted motion. An hour later, while the writers in Zaire were all still trying to figure out what had happened, the champ was happily doing magic tricks for an audience of African children.

One more source of tension becomes apparent with the consideration of boxing's milieu. Perhaps there is no athlete more courageous than a boxer, but the sport has generally been run by thugs, gamblers, and thieves who thrive on the crowd's desire to see a white man beat a black man or a black man hammer an Hispanic. The stories of boxers robbed by promoters or sacrificed by their managers are legion and too lurid for fiction. And yet, at the center of the ugly game is the single combatant, brave beyond reason as heroes must always be brave, and doomed as heroes must be doomed.

So boxing is a sport that is attractive and repulsive, hideous and funny, gross as a hammer to the head and subtle as floating like a butterfly and stinging like a bee. It is clean in the simple lines of its purpose, and dirty beyond measure in the fixes, swindles, and racism which have been present in it always. No wonder it has fascinated artists. No wonder they must take boxing on in its complexity, look the beast in the eye and smell its sweat, and see what they can make from the encounter.

Enjoy the results. Try not to hate yourself in the morning.

Alison's Game

On a sunny, September Sunday — a clearer, warmer afternoon than the morning had promised — a neighbor with a little girl who's seven, the same age as my younger daughter, called with an invitation: he had two extra tickets to the White Sox-Red Sox game. Would Alison and I like to go?

Alison said, "Yes," and the neighbor and I agreed on the ground rules: we'd leave as soon as one of the girls got antsy, no matter the inning, no matter the score.

We needn't have worried. Alison and Erin, my neighbor's daughter, brought to the game enough stuff to entertain themselves through two rainouts . . . stickers, dolls, snacks. We could have set up a shop in the grandstand.

The bonus was the game, at least if you weren't a fan of pitching. Even before we'd made our second trip to the restroom, Frank Thomas had hit two enormous homeruns for the White Sox on Tim Wakefield knuckleballs that didn't knuckle. Mo Vaughn had answered with one for Boston. Vaughn would hit another one. Thomas would hit three in his first 3 at-bats, which set-up one of the strangest dynamics I've ever seen in Fenway Park.

Though the Red Sox were behind and though the home team was still nursing a pale hope that it might make the post-season, the crowd cheered unapologetically for Thomas to whack number four. Those on hand opted for spectacle and a record over the ephemeral thrill of winning.

This was lost on Alison and Erin. When you bring stickers and doll shoes to a game, you drop them. Then you have to crawl around under your seat to find them. You can't see the ballfield from under your seat. Still, Alison was paying sufficient attention to have noticed that players on both teams were running around the bases continually. And when a multi-base Red Sox error invited two more White Sox across the plate, she looked up, took in the circling runners, and asked, "Another homerun?"

"No," I told her. "The pitcher just threw away the ball."

"Oh," she said. And then, a little wide-eyed, asked, "Do they have another one?"

As it turned out, they did, and the game went on.

Alison and Erin watched for a while, asked again who was winning, and solemnly passed the score on to their dolls, who took the bad news well.

I tried not to smile. The Red Sox were losing. It had never mattered less. As it turned out, they would rally and win the game, but that didn't turn out to matter much, either. Next season, I will attend games with Alison more often.

ϼ

Perspectives

Rick Aguilera — 34 years old, 6'4", 195 pounds — pitches for the Boston Red Sox. He used to pitch for the Twins, and before that he pitched for the Mets. Acquired by Boston a couple of months ago, he may sign-up to return next season for 3.8 million dollars. Or he may not. He said recently that part of him would like to retire and be a full-time dad.

Chris Nichting — 29 years old, 6'1", 205 pounds — was pitching for Oklahoma City the last time I looked. He used to pitch for San Antonio, and before that he pitched for Albuquerque. During his seven years in organized baseball, he's had four arm operations. The Texas Rangers have brought Nichting up to the bigs on three occasions this season. Each time it was for about 15 minutes. If anybody offers him 3.8 million dollars to pitch next season, Chris Nichting will know that person is drunk or insane.

If you want to talk to Rick Aguilera, your best bet is to make an appointment. On a hot team, he's a key player, much sought after, often mobbed. When you call his name as he walks by two hours before a game, he tends to keep on walking.

If you wanted to talk to Chris Nichting when he was working with the Rangers, you just had to show up at the ballpark and look for the guy with the wide eyes. I found him looking at the *American League Red Book* I'd left on the dugout steps when I'd gone to talk to somebody else. He was shaking his head over how many of the guys who'd been on the Texas Roster in April no longer were there. And it was only July.

For several years now, when the game has been on the line for his team, Rick Aguilera has been on the mound. He is a closer, and he's one of the best in the business. During Chris Nichting's three brief stints with the Rangers this season, when the game was on the line, Nichting was on the bench in the bullpen. For the most part, he was also there when the game wasn't on the line. When the Rangers were in Boston last month, he told me that the writers had mistaken him for three of his teammates on *that* day alone. He shrugged and smiled and said, "Nobody knows me."

When he was traded from the Twins, where he'd pitched for four years and won a World Series, Rick Aguilera was dismayed, even though he was moving from a last place team to a contender. "If you'd asked me then whether I'd sign-up for another year, I'd have said *no*," Aguilera claimed recently. "I was in a state of mind where I probably would have said I'd walk away from the game after this year."

Each time he has been called-up from Oklahoma by the Rangers, Chris Nichting has been elated. When he visited Boston, he asked me for directions from the ballpark to Harvard. "I want to see it while I'm here," he told me. "Maybe something will rub off."

He smiled when he said that, too.

Maybe he was already smart enough to know he probably wouldn't be back.

⌐⌐

EVERY SUMMER

I've talked about baseball cards before, I know that. But this is
another season, and these are new baseball cards, shiny and
stiff as new money. Each new series has its own charms and
attractions, and there are new oddities to ponder, too.

For example, why is Toronto shortstop Tony Fernandez,
perhaps the finest infielder in baseball, pictured swinging a
bat? It's not that he's a bad hitter, of course. His lifetime
average is just under .300. But a picture of him hitting? It's
sort of like a picture of Picasso mowing the lawn.

Similarly difficult to explain is the card of Red Sox third
baseman Wade Boggs. For each of the last four years, Boggs —
the American League's annual batting champion — has given
the Topps Bubble Gum and Baseball Card Company over 200
opportunities to photograph him hitting safely. Instead, they
have him staring into space in an empty ballpark, looking as if
he's trying to keep smiling even though somebody has just
poured ice water into his shoes.

As I get older, I appreciate more and more the cards of the
guys who don't look like athletes at all. San Diego pitcher
Dave LaPoint is a good example. On his '87 card, he's
apparently slouching off the mound at the end of an inning.
Maybe, it's his posture, but it looks as if his belly will drop
into the dugout several seconds before his feet reach the steps.

But the champion tank this year is Astros' reliever Aurelio Lopez. In his Houston home uniform, he looks like a monstrous bowling pin with a vertical racing stripe. He's standing on the mound with his glove raised, as if he were expecting the ball back from the catcher. But his tongue is sticking out, so maybe it's an éclair he's anticipating.

There have always been players who've seen posing for their baseball card pictures as an opportunity to have some fun. In 1969, for example, Angels infielder Aurelio Rodriguez got the Pittsburgh Pirate batboy to stand in for him. This year, Mike Mason of the Texas Rangers posed with the back of his baseball glove raised to the camera. All his fingers are in the glove except for the mischievous middle digit, which is aimed derisively at all of us silly enough to buy baseball cards.

Because each year's cards must be ready well before the season opens, there are always some inaccuracies. And each year some of them are poignant. Who'd have anticipated that Ray Knight, last year's Series MVP for the champion Mets, would be cut loose to land in Baltimore? According to his '87 baseball card, it never happened. Ray stands at third, tall and cocky in his New York uniform, confident of greater glory.

Finally, there are always cards that are just right. Pat Perry's, for example. Perry is a pitcher who may or may not be with the Cardinals by the time you read this. For the last nine years he's played seasons — or parts of seasons — in Sarasota, Daytona Beach, Columbus, Buffalo, Springfield, Arkansas, and Louisville. That's a lot of uncomfortable bus rides and disappointing cheeseburgers in pursuit of three major league wins in two brief stints with St. Louis. And yet Perry is beaming on his card.

Love is the only explanation for his tenacity and his smile, though there's no mention of love of the game on the back of Perry's card. I suppose if there were, people'd think it was maudlin. Anyway, it just says Pat "enjoys playing ping pong in his spare time."

Autumn

RECRUIT

My cousin's son Chas, a big kid, is entering his senior year as a high school student and football player. I think he still orders his priorities that way — student first; football player second — but there are those who would have it otherwise.

Like lots of high school seniors — those who play football and those who don't — Chas spent a fair chunk of time this summer traveling to colleges, trying to figure out which one he should attend. Like a lot of his athletically inclined classmates nationwide, Chas had been contacted by coaches at lots of institutions: fellows interested in enlisting his services as a Fighting Irish, a battling Bruin, or a growling Tiger. At various campuses he spoke at greater length with the coaches than with the admissions officers, which is also standard practice.

I suppose what the coaches said to him was standard practice, too, but it was dismaying, nevertheless.

At one school, a place with a fine academic reputation, an assistant coach took a look at Chas' grades — which are good — and said, "You know, son, it doesn't matter a damn to me whether you make the dean's list here. But if you play real well and we win games, I might get to keep my job and even get a raise."

At another school, a head coach cast a dubious eye on

Chas' bulk — which is considerable — and said, "When we send you home for Thanksgiving sophomore year, your momma won't recognize you, because you're gonna weigh 50 pounds more than you do now."

Chas shook his head when he told me that story. "If I put on 50 pounds, I'd fall over," he said.

"There's no way you could put on that much weight that fast without using steroids, is there?" I asked him.

"No way in the world," he said.

Happily, that coach and that school are no longer in the running for Chas' services as a player/student . . . or student/player. Neither is the school where the coach told him he wouldn't be making any scholarship offers until the Ivy League coaches culled out "the freaks of nature" — the coach's phrase for the huge, strong, fast boys who can also read and write.

Chas is a likable guy, quick to laugh — even at himself — and sharp enough to see the bozos among the coaches he's met as bozos. Would that all his blocking and tackling contemporaries could do that, too. But what a shame that they should have to.

ß

ODE TO A GOLDEN MOMENT

*"That wasn't Gerard Phelan who caught
that ball . . . God caught that ball."
"No . . . God threw it."*

Two B.C. players after The Pass

It wasn't God; He can't take sides
    When two teams come to play.
  But who's to say the gods weren't present
    On that fateful day
When Flutie spotted Phelan through
    The wet Miami air,
And, as the clock ticked down to nothing,
    Launched that final prayer?

On other days, on other fields,
    The gods have touched our games;
Established in our memories
    A small handful of names.
When Teddy Ballgame last stepped up
    To hit in Fenway Park,
The gods rode the last pitch he hit,
    That lovely, screaming arc
That ended in the bleachers while
    A small crowd stood and cheered,
And Williams, stone-faced to the last,
    Touched home and disappeared.

When Bobby Orr sailed past the crease,
    His stick high in the air,
The puck securely in the net,
    Who says the gods weren't there?

144

No Bruins fan could doubt the presence
    Of the gods that night,
Though their departure when his knees
    Went bad wrenched dark from light.

The gods outdid themselves 'round here
    In 1967 . . .
Established Fenway Park as a
    New England branch of heaven.
Until the final Series game
    They rode Yastrzemski's hip,
And then, as fickle as the seasons,
    Gave the Sox the slip.
But eight years later they returned
    With Carbo at the plate,
And that night they served notice to us;
    Sometimes they work late.
They smiled on Carlton Fisk as he
    Hopped sideways down the line,
And danced around the bases as the
    Baseball caught the twine.

John Havlicek once knew the gods,
    And they dumped him the ball;
Years later, Gerald Henderson
    Produced a curtain call,
And though when he was traded west
    It seemed at first absurd,
The gods who'd courted Gerald all
    Moved in with Larry Bird.

They've come before; they'll come again.
    Why should there be surprise
When the gods climb on a football
    Sailing through Miami's skies?
And why should we deny their present,
    Evanescent magic
As they tear lovely comedy
    from what might have been tragic?
The gods were with Doug Flutie, as
    They've been with those before him;
For a moment, frozen now it time,
    We saw the gods adore him.

145

RALLYING CRIES AND LAUGHTER

To set the stage: the Boston Red Sox, winners of the World Series in 1918 and never since, are in the middle of a west coast road trip. Mysteriously, the Sox are in first place in the American League East. But it has been thus in other years, and more often than not Boston has fumbled away its advantage in Anaheim, Oakland, or Seattle. This team of tense, history-bedeviled futilitarians should be feeling the pressure of impending collapse, wondering what new horror the baseball gods will visit upon them: what injury, or managerial gaffe, or perverse ground ball will sink them this time?

But wait.

What's going on here in the Boston dugout during the extra innings of a game in the Seattle Kingdome? Several Boston players have turned their hats backwards, and they are calling them *rally caps*.

Mike Brumley of the Mariners shouts across the field that the Boston hats are all wrong; the Seattle players turn their caps inside-out, as well as backwards. The Mariners bend the brims of their caps to create fins. Now they are land sharks.

The Sox grab bats, tape batting gloves to the ends of them, and hold them out like fishing poles.

As the top of the 12th inning opens, the Mariners cut

holes in their sanitary hose to create Mutant Ninja Turtle masks.

The Sox put Coca-Cola cups on their ears and smear shaving cream all over their faces.

Some of these men are in their late 30s. None is under 21.

This game ended when Dwight Evans homered in the 14th inning, and a relief pitcher named Daryl Irvine shut down the Mariners to win for the first time in the big leagues. After the homerun, the Sox — who were wearing their hats backwards and had cups on their ears and shaving cream all over their faces — congratulated *each other* rather than Evans.

When the game was finally over, the Mutant Ninja Turtle Mariners tipped their inside-out caps to their lunatic counterparts in the Boston dugout, as if to say, "Well, yes, tonight your magic was stronger than our magic."

Pitching, defense, and timely hitting still win baseball games. Next week any number of the Mutant Ninjas and the rally cappers may be refusing to talk to the press or demanding trades or blasting their managers for some slight, real or imagined.

No matter.

For a moment there in Seattle, the Red Sox and the Mariners reminded us that even in the dugout during a pennant race there is no rule against having a good time. If there is film of these antics, it should probably be required viewing for Little Leaguers, their parents, and their coaches.

As Willie Stargel used to put it, it is "*Play* ball" that the umpire shouts to begin the game. That's easy to forget as the ticket prices and the salaries and the advertising revenues rise; easy to forget as the pennant races come down to their final days, and we are more and more inclined to shriek with disbelief at the idiocy of this managerial decision or the hopelessness of that blunder in the field. So you in New York and Pittsburgh, you in Cincinnati and in San Francisco; you in Oakland . . . *nah*, the A's don't need it, but you in

Chicago, certainly; and you in Boston (most *definitely*, you in Boston!), try turning your TV set or your radio upside down during the next game. Try wearing your pants on your head or crossing your eyes or sticking carrots up your nose. It can't hurt . . . or it can't hurt *much*.

And it may give the disappointment that will inevitably befall most of you a little carom into absurdity, where it most certainly belongs.

☞

STEROIDS AGAIN

Last year, *Sports Illustrated* ran a chilling account of a college football player who'd used steroids until he'd finally become so crazy that nobody could talk him out of his dorm room. His parents had to come and take him home. His health was shot. He was disoriented and depressed. He couldn't concentrate. The article indicated that the youngster knew he was in real trouble the night he found himself holding a shotgun to the head of the pizza delivery man for a laugh.

Earlier this year, *The National* ran a piece about a former boxer who'd had to have his legs amputated because of the damage steroid use had done. He also testified to the psychological damage he'd suffered, including all the pain and anxiety which any addiction is likely to produce.

But steroid use is increasing anyway.

In a gym near my home, I once heard a story about a man in his early 20s who'd been hospitalized because steroids had damaged his kidneys. As soon as they let him out of the hospital, he returned to the gym and bought more steroids. That story reminded me of one I heard a while ago at the college where I teach. A colleague of mine told me about a young woman who suffered a painful eye infection from the mascara and eye make-up she'd used, and when the infection had finally cleared up, she painted the stuff on again.

"Why?" my colleague asked the girl.

"Well," she said, "I just looked so awful without it."

There's a difference in degree here, of course, but not such a difference in kind. The girl really believed she looked awful without the make-up. Our culture had taught her to believe it. And the adolescents who use steroids are victims of similar teaching. Large numbers of them are not athletes at all, of course, just growing boys who want to look bigger and stronger . . . more like the Jose Cansecos and Bo Jacksons they've been taught to admire. And the athletes too often subscribe to a lunatic athletic code which says that no act in the pursuit of winning is too extreme.

A recent book about the inside world of pro football is entitled *No Medals For Trying*. One of its main characters, New York Giants Coach Bill Parcells, won't let his trainer give the players pain-killing drugs, but he also acknowledges that he chooses not to ask how Lawrence Taylor prepared himself to play one week on a broken ankle. It turns out Taylor had liberally dosed his leg with DMSO, an anti-inflammatory agent used on horses. Why not? You get no medals for *trying* to heal or *trying* to play. The book presents Taylor as a hero for making it onto the field.

Professional, major college, and major high school athletes are under enormous pressure to perform because we have made heroes of them, and because what they do generates an enormous amount of money. Even adolescents who aren't athletes are under pressure to get bigger and stronger faster, because the advertising which comprises most of what they read or see on television has them convinced that their own perfectly normal adolescent bodies are simply not good enough. We won't change their behavior with a few horror stories as long as the gospels of *the body perfect* and *no medals for trying* continue to overwhelm by their constant presence and noise the cries of the damaged.

And our hope is not in holding up as examples places where it's done right. Notre Dame has always been celebrated as such a place, and this summer there have been charges that football players there used steroids.

Our hope is in de-emphasizing athletics until we understand athletes as performers rather than paragons.

The next and even more challenging step will be to convince our adolescents and ourselves that the human body comes in all sorts of acceptable shapes and sizes, even if the advertising industry is bound to call our efforts treason.

↢

SOX TO SEE NEW PARK

Tear down the Coliseum;
    It's beat-up and out of date;
  It's pitted and old and empty and cold
    And thoroughly second rate.
  Put up a 12-screen multiplex
    With a lobby as bright as the sun.
  Surround it with acres of parking
    For convenience, and for fun.
  Sell the space that's left to fast-food joints,
    As much as they're willing to buy.
  In the litter and noise that follow,
    We won't hear the old ghosts cry.

Spray paint the Sistine Chapel
    In contemporary tones.
  Don't worry at objections from
    The purists, or the bones
  That stir and rattle sadly in
    Confusion at the loss
  Of something that was worship-worthy:
    Fine, but, finally, dross.

Fill in the old Grand Canyon;
    Dig a deeper one next day,
  With access to the interstate
    Much closer to L.A.

If more people come, it's worth it,
    Crass as that remark may sound;
A hole's a hole, no matter where,
    No matter in which ground.
And when we build the new one
    We'll supply it with a bubble,
So folks can see it, rain or shine,
    Sans mud or other trouble,
And instead of riding mules to reach
    The river at the bottom,
We'll put in elevators made of glass . . .
    (The Hyatt's got 'em!)
And motel rooms with cable
    And Jacuzzis will await
Those who pay to ride on down
    The rock, like so much lazy freight.

The argument is money, and
    The argument's compelling;
The bottom line for baseball is —
    And has been — ticket selling.
And the Red Sox will make money if
    They tear down Fenway Park
And replace it with a pleasure dome
    That's never cold or dark.

Perhaps that's all we know and all
    We need to know as well:
It is not truth and beauty;
    It is only buy and sell.

ᕒ

GOINGS AND COMINGS

Here is what perspective means. Here is a story about time.

When Carl Yastrzemski was Roger Clemens' age, he was the guy who'd taken over left field from Ted Wolliams, and comparisons were not flattering to Yaz, who'd only hit as many as 20 home runs in five seasons. 1967, the beginning of the time of his elevation, was still two years away.

When Roger Clemens is Carl Yaztrezemski's age, Clemens will probably already have been in the Hall of Fame for several years, or so he seems to assume.

This week, Yastrzemski — at 20, a joke as Williams' replacement — is lionized for the numbers he compiled over 23 years. The Carl Yastrzemski who drew fire as the spoiled favorite of Tom Yawkey through the middle years of a career on a succession of disappointing Boston teams has faded from view. Now, and from now on, Yastrzemski is the old warrior who played forever in only one town.

Will today's transients ever believe a player who's any good would do that?

We remember him as the impossibly talented and lucky lightning rod for the team which won the pennant in 1967; the grim workman who was still leaving himself locker room notes about keeping his shoulder still at the plate in the last week of his career; the finally emotional retiree who jogged around Fenway Park on successive October afternoons, reaching out for the fans who were reaching out for him.

At 26, Roger Clemens has known similar glory. Twice a Cy Young winner, once a Most Valuable Player, he has ridden horseback like a boy-king around the ballpark . . . open-faced, open-hearted, indomitable and admired.

But look at him now. Coming off a season that has raised doubts about his endurance, he's been whining about how difficult it is to play in Boston. He and his agents have hinted that if the Red Sox can't — or won't — pay him what he feels he's worth next season, he'll demand a trade. Throughout his cryptic charges against the city or the front office or his teammates or whoever's making him unhappy, Clemens has sounded like a man whose sense of his own importance is incalculable . . . a man so thoroughly out of touch with how unfair, fickle, and perverse the world can suddenly be that he is more to be pitied than envied, no matter how many millions he will certainly earn pitching somewhere over the next few years.

Would they change places, do you think? Would Yastrzemski — whose job is done and whose place is secure — be 26 again for anything, with everything to prove? And what would Clemens give now to know that his arm will hold up and carry him past 100 to 200 and 300 wins; past the bickering over salary or his wife's seat at the park or whether the Red Sox sufficiently appreciate his clean living, and on to eminence and Cooperstown?

It astonishes me always when someone tells me he doesn't like baseball, because there's not enough going on. Think about Yastrzemski in this week of his triumph and Clemens as the deadline for salary arbitration comes on. Because it's all there. Never mind the lulls between pitches and between innings, the game's practitioners are finding out who they are and how we will regard them down the years.

₽

No Gain

Coaches tell us that they win with game plans,
    Or the brilliance of their special teams,
Or the moves of a runner who slips like a ghost
    And appears in the defense's seams.
They will say that it's all in the drafting,
    Or the way that the quarterback trains,
Or the refs, who are either against them or for them,
    Or the end with good hands when it rains.
They will celebrate kickers who still concentrate
    When the other team calls a time out,
And linemen who do their jobs, play after play,
    Whether it's a close game or a rout.

But just once in a post-game press conference,
    While the writers are poised for the word,
I'd like to hear one of those mentors concede
    There's an element of the absurd
In the game that has just been concluded;
    That the planning and work of the skilled
Men who play for our money's less vital
    Than who happened to almost get killed.
There are ligaments dangling in Cleveland,
    Even though the Browns are in first place.
And Boomer Esiason's got a bruised lung
    Or the Bengals might lead in that race.
There is cartilage afloat in New Orleans,
    Bad hamstrings have hampered the Colts,

When Washington plays, the back surgeon prays
  That Doug Williams can withstand the jolts.
And elsewhere in L.A. and Frisco,
  They're packing their mashed joints in ice,
While Steve Grogan, up in New England,
  Tries to calculate slowly, the price
Of the latest brain-stunning concussion
  He's sustained in a battered career,
And each week as we watch on the wire,
  The reports come from far and from near:
Bruised ribs, torn knees, cracked backbones, turf toe,
  Ruptured tendons, dislocated hips.
 The bodies of these men who bleed for us weekly . . .
  Collections of strains, sprains, and rips.
Well, but what the hell? They make such money —
  And they've got the off-season to heal —
So the work and the pain notwithstanding,
  It's envy you're likely to feel
Unless you've met one of them resting
  On the stairs he can't climb without pain.
Though he's just 38, had six knee operations . . .
  He's really not one to complain.
But when he wants to golf on the weekend,
  He has to plan well in advance.
He starts taking pain-killers Wednesday,
  Which gives him at least half a chance
To walk from the cart to his golf ball
  And back, when he's finished the shot
On legs that the surgeon has given up on.
  (Nothing left there to cut, trim, or knot.)
So I'd like to hear some coach acknowledge
  While the cameras and lights are still on,
That his guys have won 'cause the other team's guys
  Have been battered and broken and torn,
Separated and cracked and knocked senseless,
  Whacked and cut when they're too dazed to flee it.
I'll watch for that sometimes on Sunday,
  But I won't hold my breath 'til I see it.

157

THE IMPS OF OUR GAMES

The images of our games wink at us from unlikely places . . . or at least they wink at me.

Late this fall I spent ten days in Spain, and early in the trip I found that there, as elsewhere, the tokens and images of sports intrude like imps, even on hallowed ground. Perhaps especially on hallowed ground. At the end of one long day, I was standing in the choir of the cathedral of Barcelona, fighting cathedral narcosis, while our guide explained the carved, wooden seats as the handiwork of one John of God. A fine craftsman, John had endeavored to represent everyday scenes from the life of the 13th century in his portion of the church. The second seat from the end featured two hockey players, set to face off. I swear it. The sticks were a little too short, and the figures wore no helmets; otherwise, they might have been Blackhawks or Redwings. Who'd have thought I'd go to the cathedral in Barcelona and find hockey, eh?

A few days later, we visited a much smaller church in a much smaller town: Santo Domingo del Calzado. In a cage hung high inside this church, a chicken and a rooster both live, scratch, cluck, and crow. They are reminders of an ancient, local miracle, in which two cooked birds sprang to life on the governor's dinner table at the same time that an innocent man who'd been executed began to breathe again.

It's a splendid story. But the image in that church that snatched at my sleeve, at least metaphorically, was a life-size statue of an unidentified saint who's holding — again, I swear it — a putter. He might be a representation of Saint Seve Ballesteros of the victorious Ryder Cup, but he looks a lot older than that: several hundred years older.

A day later, on a long, dry bus ride to Segovia, I was still puzzling over the hockey players and the golfing saint when another image no less powerful appeared outside the dirty window. Alongside the highway, bordered all the way to the horizon by barren dirt and the Spanish equivalent of sage brush, was a perfect, emerald green soccer field. Of course, it must have been irrigated . . . but where were the water pipes out there? The bus rumbled on, and the field was gone.

An hour later, in Segovia, the rest of the tour group marveled at the Roman aquaduct. I feigned interest. But my mind was still on that impossible field of soccer dreams . . . built — in the desert — so that who would come? What celestial team of the heavenly talented? And how did one know where to buy a ticket? Or when they would play?

ﭖ

BO JACKSON

Most of the people who've commented on the Bo Jackson story have missed the point. It's no sin to change your mind. no matter how vehemently you've announced that you'd never do it. Writers who dutifully reported that Bo Jackson was committed exclusively to baseball shouldn't feel personally betrayed.

Jackson has alienated both his teammates on the Royals and his perspective teammates on the Raiders, not to mention future opponents. The baseball players are bitter, because their contracts stipulate that they can't play anything more dangerous than bridge in the off-season, while the Royals will apparently let Jackson play pro football. The football players are pumped up, red-eyed, and meaner than usual, because Jackson had the brass to characterize *their* game as his hobby. But these stories are tangential to the real issue, too.

Jackson's intention to play two pro sports has set historians to checking the records of others who've tried it, and the solemn consensus is that — in these days of designer, year-round, specific sport conditioning programs, extended seasons, and linemen the size of battleships — no mere mortal can handle the demands of football *and* baseball for money. But even that stuffy contention misses the mark, too.

The heart of the matter here is that a young man has gone

insane. Apparently without coercion, he has announced his intention to diminish a sensible life in the game of spring and summer in order to dabble in the rumble and crunch of the game of blitzes, bombs, and forearm shivers. He has the opportunity to spend his working days playing a *genuine* game in which a pitcher only rarely tries to hurt or even frighten a batter (and given the regularity with which Bo Jackson strikes out, no pitcher in *his* right mind would throw at him, so his health is safe in baseball), but he wants to augment this pleasant life by giving 11 men the opportunity to try to tear his legs apart and shatter his ribs with every snap of the ball.

Baseball players have nicknames like *Ducky* and *Rooster,* while football players have nicknames like *Mean Joe* and *The Assassin.* Retired baseball players strut their stuff in old timers' games, hit lazy fungo flies, or happily chatter from coaches' boxes coast to coast. Retired football players lurch around on fused knees, trading war stories through their broken teeth.

Yet, unaccountably, Bo Jackson, safe in the bosom of the game of life renewed, wants to tempt the death sport.

The real story here is tragic. A young man has come unglued. It's not such a bad thing to *change* a mind, but what a sad thing to *lose* one.

THE GAME

The Elis have lost more than they've won,
    And Harvard has done just the same,
So will anyone really be watching,
    When they hook up again in The Game?

It's hardly Miami and Penn State.
    You'll see very few future pros
If you wander by that colliseum
    Near the banks where the Charles River flows.
But you can count the seats that are empty
    On the fingers of one lonely hand
When the Yales and the Harvards play football,
    Though it's only the Ivy League brand.

Maybe *only's* a qualification
    That needs to be qualified more:
In the Ivys, most players are students,
    And the backs don't get paid when they score.
The linemen are somewhat less monstrous
    Than their counterparts in the Big 10,
And the Ivy League champ gets no bowl bid,
    Despite more bowls than *ever* have been.

But the Harvards and Yales have tradition
    That Miami and Penn couldn't buy
If each robbed its athletic department
    Of the dough in the scholarship pie.

That's 'cause Harvard and Yale've played a hundred two times
    Since before there was even TV . . .
  Since before college teams were the farm clubs
    For the NFL on NBC.
  And The Game's formed the backdrop for writers
    Damon Runyun and F. Scott Fitzgerald . . .
  And that didn't stop with the 30s and 40s,
    George Plimpton's a more recent herald.
So the crowd is all doctors and lawyers,
    And industry captains galore,
  Hot shot politicians and movers and shakers.
    Who knows who's left minding the store?
  And when one team is trouncing the other,
    There's no scoreboard to start shooting rockets,
  But the fans on the winning team's side of the field
    Take their handkerchiefs out of their pockets,
  And they wave them across at the losers,
    And they sing *Boola, Boola* or something,
  And you'd have to attend 'bout a thousand games elsewhere
    To ever see any more dumb thing.
Maybe that's why The Game's still important
    To the whole football world, because really
  In a hollow sport sold out to TV and profit,
    There should *still* be a place for the silly.

TOO BAD TO FIGHT

It's ironic on a number of levels that Mike Tyson's indictment for rape should have resulted in calls for the postponement of his November fight with Heavyweight Champion Evander Holyfield. Is Tyson no longer sufficiently virtuous to try to kill someone in the ring?

There are, of course, many reasons to cancel rather than postpone all prize fights, and they've all been compelling for years. Boxing damages its practitioners beyond repair. It blinds them and hammers their kidneys to pulp. It beats them stupid. In too many cases to document, it even robs them of money, which is one excuse the game's supporters give for their backing. "Boxing is the way out of the ghetto for the minority kids," they claim. But for every rare Floyd Paterson, who offers evidence for that contention, there are thousands of battered losers.

It's bad enough to be conned into practicing basketball all day at the expense of learning to read and write, because you're sure you'll make millions in the NBA and you can hire someone to read and write for you. How much worse to be conned out of your wits? At least basketball players who don't make it can go back to school. Too many boxers who don't make it have nowhere to go but the clinic or the emergency room.

Mike Tyson, of course, did make it in the sense that too often matters most. He made money. But by most accounts the titles of *Champion* and *Former Champion* have only aggravated his previous inclination toward violence and ugliness outside of the ring.

Should Mike Tyson be allowed to fight? Maybe he should *only* be allowed to fight. And if he is found guilty of this latest charge, some of what he earns can be siphoned-off to pay the victim of his crime, since that is one way we measure guilt and make reparation. And an additional portion might be ear-marked for the former boxers who can no longer see or hear or think. Deduct enough from Mike Tyson's paycheck, and the Don Kings of the world will fall away from him. Keep deducting, and before too long the alleged sport itself will shrivel up and die.

It's a large dream to build upon one indictment in the Superior Criminal Court of Marion County in Indiana, but wouldn't it be a shame to let all the agitation in favor of the postponement or the cancellation of a heavyweight fight go to waste?

And let it not be said that the alleged victim in Mike Tyson's most recent alleged assault has been forgotten in such a plan. For her courage in coming forward to do battle in court with Tyson the Heavyweight, she would no doubt go down in history as the individual who knocked out boxing.

ß

Rebecca Lobo

I worked Friday. Though lots of people get a couple of days off for Thanksgiving, there was no help for it. We had a program to produce.

I'm not complaining. But it means that my wife has had our two daughters on her hands in raw weather since the middle of Wednesday — when school let out after a half day — with assistance from me only on Thursday . . . Well, you get the point.

So, I'm taking Amy and Alison on Sunday. We're going to the Fleet Center (which has just this year replaced the Boston Garden) for as much of a college basketball double-header as the kids might enjoy. It's a double-header of women's games. In game one, UCLA meets Vanderbilt; in game two, Ohio State plays Boston College. Tip-off for the first tilt is 1:00 PM, but Amy, Alison, and I will be courtside an hour and a half before that, because Rebecca Lobo — she of last season's undefeated National Championship Team from the University of Connecticut and this year's U.S. National Team — will be hosting a clinic.

Will Amy (age 10) and Alison (age 6) learn to go to their left, head fake, and double pump? It's unlikely. But there is this other, more important matter that I'm always trying to address.

Sometimes when I'll be watching a baseball or a basketball game on television, Amy or Ali will wander into the room, check out the game for a minute or two, then ask: "Do girls play this, too?"

I can always tell them "yes," but at the Fleet Center on Sunday I can show them. Or, more accurately, Rebecca Lobo can show them. They will see right away that she is tall and strong, comfortable and confident in her athlete's body. They will see that she smiles easily and often; that she looks you in the eye when she answers your questions and thinks before she answers them.

If they'd been with me when I interviewed her last winter, when Lobo was still in school, they'd have seen that she talked with as much enthusiasm about some of her classes as she did about the success of the basketball team, evidence that she had not let dedication to a game bend her life away from everything else.

I can tell my children that all these qualities are significant, and I do. But it won't hurt for Rebecca Lobo to personify the message, too.

At the end of last year's college basketball season, Rebecca Lobo was the most-celebrated female player in the land. The several dozen most-celebrated male players are working for splendid wages in the NBA these days. I have to acknowledge that I'm glad — backward as it may sound — that there is no comparable opportunity for young women quite yet.

If there were, Rebecca Lobo most certainly wouldn't be available to Amy and Alison and the rest of the girls and boys who will meet her and learn from her on Sunday.

℞

PROFESSIONAL SPORTS

Apparently during the process of deciding against another run for the presidency, former Senator Eugene McCarthy recently said, "Being in politics is like being a football coach. You have to be smart enough to understand the game and dumb enough to think it's important."

I like that contention, because it deflates football coaches, whom too many folks deify. It also demonstrates that at least one presidential type can step into the world of sports — or at least allude to it — without making an ass of himself.

Consider Gerald Ford, who used to bounce golf balls off the coconuts of people careless enough to be in his vicinity on the course. Ford was a football player when he was a student at Michigan; it earned him only jokes about how he must have played too long without his helmet.

Ford's predecessor, Richard Nixon, fared even worse when he dabbled in sports. Reporters used to ask Nixon whether he had been moved or disconcerted or in any way touched by the huge anti-war demonstrations outside the White House during the late 60s and early 70s. Nixon would claim that he hadn't been aware of them, because he was watching the Washington Redskins on TV. Nor was that the height of his arrogance. On at least one occasion, he sent a play to Redskins' Coach George Allen, though there is no proof that he threatened to draft the coach and send him to Viet Nam if he didn't use it in a game.

Ronald Reagan didn't have much luck when he bumbled into sports talk, either. Despite his early experience as a baseball broadcaster, President Reagan was known to confuse Grover Cleveland (a fat and happy former Chief Executive) with Grover Cleveland Alexander (a hugely successful, though alcoholic, pitcher).

And then, there's George Bush. His idea of an afternoon of sport is to roar around aimlessly off the Maine coast in the sort of power boat favored by Miami drug runners. This is a falling off that's near tragic, since Bush used to be a fair baseball player. When he was captain of the Yale team he shook the hand of Babe Ruth. He should have quit while he was ahead.

Maybe some of this sports-oriented foolishness can stand as metaphor for what all these guys did when they weren't playing or talking about our games. If so, it's a shame that Mr. McCarthy realizes just how dumb he'd have to be to seek again the job Messrs. Nixon, Ford, Reagan, and Bush have held.

℞

FOOLING 'EM

Somehow, it's right it's come down to this:
    We get to depend on a fluke . . .
  A pitch that bobs on the air like a kite.
    Look, this is no rebuke

Of the knuckleball Tim Wakefield pushes,
    Fast as fluttering leaves,
  While the Sox are a game from vacation
    And while every Sox fan grieves

The losses out in Cleveland
    And hopes for a better day,
  Or maybe two, and maybe three . . .
    And then they go all the way.

But first, we depend on a squirrelly pitch
    That hovers and floats and darts
  And looks to hitters like they could hit it,
    And then it breaks their hearts.

Or else it comes in flat as Kansas,
    Sits there, big as a plate,
  Then drops like a bowling ball out of a plane
    And everyone swings too late

And looks like a chump who should have retired
    The night before the game,
  'Cause when three knuckleballs drop for strikes
    No two ever look the same.

It's right it should all come down to the knuckleball.
    I'll tell you why. There's a reason.
  From April to now this campaign's been
    A knuckleball of a season.

The strike, replacement players,
    Clownish owners, wild cards, yes . . .
  A lot of life-long baseball fans
    Declared the game a mess

They didn't need and turned to
    Other ways to pass the time . . .
  And called the players names involving
    Words I cannot rhyme

In a family piece (you get the point.)
    The season looked lost and dead,
  But it fluttered to life like a knuckleball
    And stood misery on its head

And filled the hearts of Sox fans with
    The joy contention brings:
  The dreams of titles, pennants, champagne,
    And World Series rings,

All hopes about as goofy as a
    Knuckleball in flight.
  That's why it's only perfect that
    At 8 o'clock tonight

The season should come down to Wakefield,
    Down to his knuckleball,
  Which fools 'em, or it doesn't,
    As I do — as do we all.

CLOSING DAY

On each Opening Day we remember all the other Opening Days. Everybody knows that. The center of comedy is, "Here we all are again," and that is also the message of Opening Day. The other charms of the occasion are evident and obvious, too. Nothing has gone wrong yet. The most woeful club can theoretically go 162-0.

But closing days have their charm, as well.

On a long-gone Sunday afternoon in September, years before I moved to Boston, I was visiting friends here, and we were watching the Red Sox on television. They were out of it, as they have been down the stretch this season. They were playing game one of a double-header. (That's how long ago it was!) Somebody suggested that we should drive to the ballpark to see the second game, and we did.

Nobody thought about bringing a jacket. We sat in the bleachers. It must have already been cool by the time we got there, and by the time we'd sat through a couple of innings, it was cold.

Maybe Bart Giamatti was there, too. Maybe that was the very day at the ballpark about which he later wrote: "It breaks your heart. It is designed to break your heart. The game begins in the spring, when everything else begins again, and it blossoms in the summer, filling the afternoons and

172

evenings, and then as soon as the chill rains come, it stops and leaves you to face the fall alone."

I don't remember rain that day, but I remember the chill, all right. I remember that it came as a surprise. I remember that everybody else wanted more beer after the game, and I wanted coffee.

But rain and chill are only part of the fun of the closing days, and here I am not talking about one-game playoffs, the two (soon to be six) pre-World Series matchups, or the Serious itself. Any idiot with a television set and the capacity to stay up past midnight for a few weeks can appreciate those. I'm talking about the games — sometimes half a season's worth and sometimes only a few — which the play-by-play guys refer to when they talk about "playing out the string." These are games which do not matter in the standings, but they are as full as any others of the images of baseball which we need to carry us through the winter and into the spring, when the comedy will begin again.

Consider, as evidence, Rich Gedman, and my favorite image of him. Most Boston fans remember the large, good-natured local as a two-time All-Star catcher who had the misfortune to collaborate with Bob Stanley in the creation of a pitch that got away at the most unfortunate moment imaginable in game six of the 1986 World Series. *I* remember that night, too. But because I go to the closing days which do not matter to anybody but a few of us, I also remember Rich Gedman in a late September game that preceeded by five years the catcher's darkest moment and the subsequent unraveling of his career in Boston. I remember his hitting a late-inning double out of a batter's box covered in the autumn shadow. It was a stand-up double, and after Gedman had chugged out the hit, he stood on second base and raised his fist over his head and did just the first, tentative step of a little dance, like Rocky at the top of those stairs in Philadelphia. I watched him and thought, "There's a baseball player who gets some fun out of the game."

On another day among the closing days, this one several years before the Gedman double, I didn't get to the ballpark until the game was well underway. The ticket booths were closed, either because the men who were supposed to be in them had stepped-in to see the game, or because they'd grown tired of the whole business and gone home. When I finally got the attention of a fellow beyond the turnstyles, he shook his head and shrugged in the direction of the locked ticket booths. But further down Yawkey Way at the service gate, I found another man in uniform with fewer scruples. He couldn't sell me a ticket, either, and he shrugged, too, but he shrugged in the direction of the ballfield and said, "What the hell? Go on in."

I thanked him and walked straight for the nearest tunnel to the field. At the other end of it, Butch Hobson knelt in the on-deck circle, searching the pitcher's face and his motion for a clue that would enable Butch to kick his average up from .259 to .260. Again, the Red Sox were out of it. In a normal tone of voice I could have said, "Tough year, Butch," and he'd have heard me.

What is there to see in the closing days this season? Only the unobservant need ask. There is the peculiar — persistent, if sporadic — presence of Steve Lyons to appreciate. Over the meaningless days, this delightful career bad penny of a ballplayer keeps bouncing out of the dugout, a pinch runner eager to score, whether it matters or not. There is Tony Pena, who has reached the end of the line with a good deal less fanfare than Nolan Ryan or George Brett, but who is no less entitled to our attention. For several years on this club, he has laughed when nobody else would.

On every team but a very few, some of the famous and many of the obscure have been playing out their last days before gatherings sometimes too small to be called crowds while the weather turns. If you can't find the poignancy in that circumstance, whether those on the cusp of departing the game are veteran millionaires or utility men who have only just arrived in the show, you won't be able to feel the full pleasure of the day next April when the gates open again on a team that — statistically, at least — has a shot.

In my office, there are images of two old ballplayers. The first is Babe Ruth. He is sitting on a dugout bench which has been covered with a blanket. He wears a heavy brown overcoat and a cap, and he has on leather gloves. Between two of the fingers of his left hand he's holding a cigar, which he has apparently forgotten. He is staring out at a ball field. The other is Willie Mays. He is on the cover of *The Sporting News*, and he's wearing the uniform of the New York Mets, the team with which he spent the only bad years of his career — the last two. The headline above him reads: *Willie Mays Calls It A Day*.

These are both images of the fall, and the remarkable thing is that the expressions on the faces of Ruth and Mays are identical. Both men are astonished that the game is going on without them. How can this be happening? They are baffled. To them, it looked like forever. They paid insufficient attention to the closing days until it was too late.

ᚹ

WORLD SERIES, 1993

If you root for the Phils, your Budweiser spills,
    And there's change buried deep in your couch.
  You're behind on your rent, and your rear axle's bent;
    When you stub your toe, you don't say *Ouch!*

You say all sorts of things that the radio can't,
    And on some nights you don't feed the cat.
  You forget, or you figure she can feed herself.
    You and she are both running too fat.

If you root for the Jays, you've found numerous ways
    To bring order to all that you do.
  You never forget what you've left at the cleaners,
    You don't own an unpolished shoe.

Your desk is uncluttered, your checkbook is balanced,
    Your garbage cans all have tight lids.
  Your pedigreed golden retriever is smart,
    And plays gently with both of your kids.

The kids of all Phillies fans eat dirt and paste
    And have no use for teachers or school,
  While the offspring of all of the Blue Jays' supporters
    Wear dresses or ties, and don't drool.

The fans of the Jays — many of them — speak Spanish
    And French, also Latin and Greek;
  The fans of the Phils can sometimes manage English,
    That is, those of them who can speak.

Most of them only grunt on their most vocal days,
    Scratch themselves, spit, and paw at the ground,
  While the Jays fans play classical music and chess
    And pass *paté de foie gras* around.

Pretty silly, I know, but a lot of folks feel
    That there's some truth in these goofy theories.
  They are people (how *strange!*) who can't find enough fun
    In the simple playing of the World Series.

NUMBER 28: DEFENSE/TENOR SAX

Last week I drove down to Rhode Island to watch the U.S. Women's Olympic ice hockey team play a tune-up against Providence College.

It wasn't much of a game. The Providence Team is always very strong. In fact, nine current members of the Olympic team played at Providence. But their regular season hasn't begun. Providence isn't game-ready. The members of the national team have been playing together for months, and they're in superb condition. They scored early and often. I stopped counting when the score reached 10 – zip.

Or I lost count. I'm not sure which, because at several points during the game I found myself searching the ice for a particular Providence player named Jennifer Bill. She is 5'3" tall. I learned that from the program. She is a sophomore, and she is a Music major. I know this, because — before the game began — she was the one who played the national anthem.

She played it on a saxophone about half as tall as she is. And, of course, while she played it she was wearing her hockey uniform. So, she was bulky — top to bottom — and the sweet, solemn sound of the sax — played with precision and without flourishes — flowed away from her and dipped and swelled and settled on the sparse crowd in the arena.

Well beyond the end of the anthem and into the game,

and then beyond the game and into the solitary drive back home, I found myself wishing for one of the few times since I've started working in radio that I was working for a newspaper instead. As a print reporter, I might have had a photographer with me at that game, and now I might have a picture, black and white, of the hockey player and her saxophone.

And I found myself wondering how many Division I male athletes are Music majors. And than I found myself wondering whether — when my daughters become college sophomores — I'd rather have them be varsity hockey players, or musicians so confident and cool that they can stand on skates in a bulky hockey uniform and play sweetly. Because it seems beyond all reason to dream that they — or anyone — could be both.

CRYING TIME AGAIN
(THIS TIME IN CLEVELAND)

Long faces in the dog pound,
   Where the Browns supporters dwelt
And donned dumb dog masks, yipping,
   Barking . . . In those seats it's felt
That Art Model betrayed the fans
   Who sat through rain and sleet,
And filled his ugly stadium
   And bought up every seat . . .
Which wasn't, as it turned out, quite
   Enough to match the money
Model could make in Baltimore,
   The place where (this is funny)
The Colts once played, until they left,
   To take a better deal,
Which made Colts fans feel bad *then*,
   And it's how the Browns fans feel
Right *now*. But I've no sympathy
   For fans of either group.
For each I have a message. Ready?
   Okay, here's the scoop:
The owners are all businessmen;
   The players entertainers.
Both choose to fill their wallets:
   Easy choices, real no-brainers.

If you choose to regard them as
    Belonging where they are,
You've only got yourself to blame
    When they blow town to star
On someone else's playground,
    Built by someone else's gelt;
It's been that way at least
    Since '57, when folks felt
That when the Dodgers flew west out
    Of Brooklyn there would form
A rain of locusts, clouds of doom,
    At least a firestorm.
It didn't happen. Life went on,
    Although somewhat diminished,
But the phrase *home team* rang hollow
    Then, and maybe now it's finished.

If you would still call some
    Collected ballplayers your own
Because they temporarily
    Play ball close to your home,
Because you've bought their caps or,
    In their losing, helped them grieve,
You probably deserve to have
    Your heart cracked when they leave.

KEEPING SCORE

There are various ways to measure the popularity of individual sports, but certainly money is the most convenient. It's also one of the most revealing. *Forbes Magazine* recently listed the 30 most highly paid athletes in the world. Though the designation *athlete* is sometimes suspect, the results provide great fodder for discussion and debate.

Mike Tyson, boxing's most visible warrior if no longer its champion, leads the list with $28.6 million: $27 million of that total comes to him for his work in the ring, which means he makes $1.6 million for endorsing something. Buster Douglas, who dethroned Tyson as champ, makes a million for endorsing something, too, and I don't know what *that* is, either. Anyway, Douglas is second on the list.

You have to go to number eight to find someone who plays one of what most consider the Big Four pro sports: baseball, football, basketball, and hockey. It is Michael Jordan, and if there isn't a little sneaker-shaped asterisk by his name, there should be. He makes three times his $2-million-a-year salary for lending his name to various products.*

The remaining spots among the Top 10 athlete/earners are filled by two more boxers, three auto racers, and two

* *Editor's note: Isn't this quaint? In 1997, Michael Jordan had a one-year, $30 million contract just to play basketball.*

golfers. I hadn't heard of any of the auto racers, which is certainly no knock against them. Each makes about a million dollars a year endorsing things: motor oil and life insurance, I guess.

Actually, my favorite among the top ten on this list is Arnold Palmer, who sits comfortably at number nine. According to *Forbes*, Arnie is making a crummy hundred grand a year at golf, but he makes $8 million more as a clothes horse and tractor jockey on TV . . . more evidence that it's a great country.

The first woman doesn't show up on the list until number 13, where we find Steffi Graf. She makes a little over a million dollars a year playing tennis, and another five million renting her name and her face to advertisers. She ranks just behind Boris Becker in these categories, and a few hundred grand above Andre Agassi, Ivan Lendl, and Stefan Edberg. Feminists who despair that Ms. Graf only ranks 13th on the list will perhaps be encouraged that at least she's edged those guys out.

The first baseball player on the list is José Canseco, who makes $5.5 million a year to play baseball and another half a million talking about it on his 900 phone line or endorsing things. (I don't know.) This is the same guy who joked about needing a bodyguard with an Uzi.

I don't want the tone of all this to suggest that I think money is everything. In fact, I have another list that proves the contrary. About the same time the *Forbes* top 30 appeared, *Fortune Magazine* announced that there were three billionaires among the owners of the big league baseball teams: Atlanta's Ted Turner, Montreal's Charles Bronfman, and Detroit's Tom Monaghan. One of 'em won a pennant once* . . . just one. Despite the bucks, the others are still chasing the dream.

⚑

---

* *Editor's note: Another quaint statistic, as it turns out. Ted Turner's Braves went on to win a lot of division championships and pennants, not to mention the World Series . . . one of the risks of skepticism for any writer.*

TWILIGHT TIME

In the *New York Times* on Sunday, nestled among the basketball stories and the football stories and the hockey stories was a forlorn item. The headline read, *Quietly, the DH May Be on the Way Out.* The DH, of course, is the designated hitter rule, which enables teams in the American League to include in their line-ups a man who doesn't play in the field. The DH customarily hits instead of the pitcher.

It seems that some of the owners of baseball teams have noticed that designated hitters tend to make a lot of money for being what they might term half-players. In 1990, the average salary for the seven players who were designated hitters for 80 games or more was $1,142,143. A statistic like this carries more weight than all the philosophical and historical arguments against the designated hitter — at least among the people who pay the freight — and the thinking seems to be that perhaps one day in the not-too-distant future, the American League will lay the 10th player to rest.

This would delight baseball purists who argue that the presence of the designated hitter oversimplifies the manager's job and fouls up comparisons between pitchers in the American League, who have to face nine *bona fide* hitters, and their counterparts in the National League, who get to pitch to each other three or four times a game.

But like all questions worth considering, this business of whether or not the DH should endure is more complicated than it might seem. Argue — as traditionalists do — that baseball shouldn't change, or that — as the owners say — a million dollars a year is an awful lot of money to pay a guy who doesn't have to play in the field and you miss the human face of this most compassionate of baseball's innovations.

Think about Orlando Cepeda. By the time he was 36, his knees were so hopelessly shot that he could not run enough even to play first base. In 1972, he played a total of 31 games, all but three of them for Atlanta in the National League. He was, apparently, washed up. But in 1973, upon the dawning of the designated hitter rule in the American League, Orlando Cepeda was reborn. He joined the Red Sox and hit .289 with 45 extra base hits. Among his singles were 30 or 40 shots off the wall that would have been doubles for anyone else, but so what? The DH should have been called *The Cepeda Rule*.

It has often been thus since. Lots of battered, old worthies have been kept off the card show circuit for another season or so by this rule which recognizes that being able to hit — never mind that you can no longer run or throw or field — is a very fine thing: something to which attention must be paid.

The players reclaimed and redeemed by this proviso have often been grateful for their jobs and more pleasant to the writers than any of their cocky, multi-talented teammates. Designated hitters are at the end of the line, and they know it. They don't tend to be in a hurry. They are often flattered that you are interested in them at all. Someone should do a study to find out if players who get to be designated hitters before they retire altogether make the transition to life after baseball more easily. We could see if the twilight time of designated hitting has helped them to accept their own limitations and proceed with more dignity and balance into a world in which they must make their own plane reservations and pay for their bubble gum.

Think on all this, you owners, before you vote your

pocketbooks. And before you dismiss this defense of the designated hitter as merely the babble of a soft-hearted writer with no particular expertise to bring to the debate, consider that this particular writer knows firsthand the sweet second chance of the designated hitter. With his one bad knee and one much worse, he would have been out of disorganized baseball years and years ago had the DH rule not somehow trickled all the way down to the Cambridge, Massachusetts Municipal League, B West Division.

ʀ

THE THANKSGIVING DAY GAME

It was just a mile's walk to the movie theater, where we'd all
    meet,
Having left our houses by 9, because by 2 we would be eating
Our separate Thanksgiving turkeys, around our separate tables,
Our memories filled with visions of the big kids, muscles tight
    as cables,
As they'd performed their homecoming heroics for the town,
And for their old and famous coach, and for the cheers that
    they called down
From the wooden seats filled up with everyone we knew.
From behind the movie theater we followed the railroad track
    through
The woods, though we'd been told a hundred times not to,
And before we could see the field we could see the cold blue
Sky over it, and hear the odd rumble of the bass drum and
    people crowded together
At this crazy time of day in the morning, and hear the leather
Slap against the hands of the quarterbacks and the ends,
And one of us had a brother on the team, and so his friends
Could squeeze into the first row of seats along the home team
    side.
But not for long. Restless, we'd climb the bleachers and slide
Along the railings and shout at each other and buy forbidden
    candy
Apples, and hot dogs, and peanuts, and orange soda . . . all
    dandy

187

Things to eat once a year in the morning at a game scheduled
at ten for fear
That otherwise it would conflict with Thanksgiving, the
biggest dinner of the year.
And so we ran and crunched the cinders underneath our
sneakers,
And raced on to the field at halftime to test our weaker
Arms against those of the heroic players. The boys who had
been us
Lounged against the rails along the stands, and watched the
cheerleaders, and cussed:
And the men who had been them asked their wives in scarves
if they were too cold,
And dug their hands into the pockets of their tweed
sportcoats, and felt the tug of being old
Enough to worry about whether they would have to leave
early
If their wives were weary, or the baby cried, or the wind
turned surely.
And then the game, which was the center of the day, would
begin again,
And into the afternoon the biggest, strongest boy, who could
be comfortable with men,
Would take the ball and run past a boy who'd misread the
play
And zigged when he should have zagged and would remember
Thanksgiving day
Forever as the time he blew it, and allowed the winning
touchdown.
And the hopeless, muffled band would play, and the
cheerleaders tumble around
The field in their wool sweaters, and grin and laugh at each
other
Harder than any football game could account for. And the
grandmothers
At home would look at the clock, and despair that the turkey
would dry out
But by then we would be back on the tracks, headed home,
with no doubt

In our little minds that when we got there the bird would be
     brown and hot,
And the potatoes buttered and fluffy, and cranberry sauce,
     which was not
For any day other than Thanksgiving, like the morning
     football game
That brought the whole town out to shout up into the
     November sky
At what we would be, or had been, and remember now with
     thanks in the mind's eye.

MUHAMMAD ALI

Each fall the Center for the Study of Sport in Society at Northeastern University holds a banquet to celebrate the accomplishments and contributions of some number of athletes, coaches, and others connected with our games. One feature of the festivities is the induction of one or more worthies into the Center's Hall of Fame. It's always a happy occasion, but each honoree faces an unhappy prospect: inevitable comparison with the Center's first inductee, Muhammad Ali.

No matter that some of us think the sport of which Muhammad Ali was the three-time champion should be abolished. This champion long ago transcended the limits of the world of boxing. Prize fighting gave him his international platform, but he has earned honors such as his induction into various halls of fame by virtue of the way he has used that platform. He may have been the greatest heavyweight boxer in history; certainly, he was the most imaginative. But his attraction only began with his talent. As a very young man, a new champion, he announced that pride in himself and his race compelled him to change his name and his creed. He endured the outrage and ridicule of a press and public that either resented his courage and his vision, or had no idea what he was up to.

When his government tried to draft him into the military, he spontaneously cried, "I got no quarrel with them Viet Congs," which was enough to make him a hero in some quarters. Then, given time to reflect on his circumstances, Muhammad Ali — the converted Muslim — said, "I pray five times a day for peace. How can I go to war?"

That should have won over everyone else, but it didn't.

Muhammad Ali lost his license to fight. Then he lost three years of his youth to the process which ended only when the Supreme Court vindicated him. When it was all over, he could have sued most of the nation's boxing commissions. He sued no one. He said, "This is not about money."

This is not to suggest that Muhammad Ali has been a saint. He was so improbably loud as a young man that he shakes his head now and says of himself, "I was crazy." In at least some of his fights — most notably the bout against Ernie Terrill — he was gratuitously vicious. The rhetoric with which he hammered Joe Fraser before their fights was insulting even by boxing's standards.

But Muhammad Ali has also been generous and great-hearted in circumstances that might have driven lesser men to self-pity. Persecution for his color and his religion only made him stronger. "Standing up for my religion made me happy," he has said. "It was no sacrifice." For a generation of men and women, white and black, who hated racist hypocrisy and their helplessness against the war, Muhammad Ali became a symbol of hope and triumph more powerful than all but a very few.

He fought too long, of course. Of boxers that almost goes without saying. He suffers now from Parkinson's Syndrome, which has robbed him of his quick tongue, but his faith has provided him with wisdom, and his wit is intact.

In Thomas Hauser's excellent biography of Ali a few years ago, the Champ said that his affliction was God's will, because the result of it has been that people did not envy him, which is good. Envy might prevent them from hearing and accepting his message of peace. He has traveled around the world again and again to deliver that message. He appears at the Olympics and the NBA playoffs, but across Africa and Indonesia they also chant his name. His journey has taught us something about how to make a meaningful life in this slippery world.

ᚱ

WINTER

WINTER'S COMPENSATION

If you don't think about how cold it's going to get, there are things to look forward to in the winter. This is even if you don't ski, and you live on a hill that's the very last place that the town plows.

Consider, for example, skating lessons for the kids. This winter, my kids will go together fairly early Saturday morning. It will get them away from the TV, and — even if no other good things happened — that would be sufficient cause to sign-up again and again.

But other good things do happen. My younger daughter (almost 5) will try skating for the first time this season. I'm looking forward to it, because for the past two winters I've watched my older daughter get a little more comfortable and a little more confident on the ice each week.

This is not to say that there are necessarily any future Nancy Kerrigans or Brian Boitanos or Ray Bourques out there. In fact, there have always seemed to me to be more goofballs than anything else. The last thing that all the kids learn is how to stop, and many of them — especially, the boys — seem to put it off intentionally, because they enjoy crashing themselves into the boards. The adults — wrapped around their paper coffee cups — cringe at each *thud!* But the kids just laugh, struggle to their feet, and do it again. Nobody gets hurt. Helmets are required, and everybody's bundled-up. In their snowsuits and peering over scarves, the littlest skaters are about as agile as fireplugs . . . and about as fast.

But it *is* cold.

The lessons are in an outdoor rink with green canvas sides that buzz and snap in the wind, and sometimes the kids whine. Some parents exhort their children to be tough.

"Only 10 minutes left in your lesson," they shout. "Keep skating!"

Not me. Last year and the year before that, if my older daughter came painfully pumping and almost gliding her way out of the pack to tell me that her feet were frozen, I walked with her into the little, heated shed, helped her take off her skates, and rubbed her feet until she could feel her toes again. Then, if there was any lesson time left, she'd go back out and skate a little more. If not, we headed home. We listened to the acoustic music station on the car radio, sometimes singing along, and she'd ask what was for lunch.

This time around, I'll be taking both daughters. The littler one will gradually discover that she can stand on skates and that she can glide a little, and eventually that she can chase her sister. That much I know, but there's much to discover.

Maybe the two of them will push each other, and both will stay out on the ice through the whole, cold lesson. Maybe I'll be rubbing two sets of feet.

Probably on the way home, one of them will scrape the sludge off her skates and hit the other one in the eye with it. Almost certainly, they'll argue over who has to sit in the back, and maybe they won't want to listen to the same radio station.

But maybe on some mornings, we'll all decide to sing.

TRAVIS ROY

One week ago, Travis Roy — a 20-year-old Boston University freshman — banged headfirst into the boards during his very first shift in the BU hockey team's opening game. He fell away from the boards and onto the ice in an impossibly awkward way: his neck was broken and his spinal cord was bruised. He had no feeling in his arms or legs. Nobody who saw it happen or who has seen the videotape of the fall — which the local TV stations have ghoulishly persisted in playing and replaying — is likely to forget it.

We have been trained to take for granted a considerable level of balance and grace in our athletes, and an athlete whose spinal column has been crushed has none of either when he falls.

What Travis Roy eventually will have remains to be seen. Early this week, surgeons relieved the pressure on his bruised nerves and rebuilt the fourth vertebra, broken in the accident. Perhaps, like the most fortunate victims of spinal cord injury, Roy will regain some use of his arms and legs.

On our answering machine on Monday, the first caller responding to Travis Roy's injury urged *Only A Game* to attribute the accident to the violence inherent in ice hockey as the sport is taught and played today. It was a shot at an explanation, and had Travis Roy been a prize fighter, it would have worked. Or if he'd been hurt by some goon who'd clubbed him to the ice with a stick, or jumped on his neck and broken it, it would have been an easy call. But Roy was injured in the context of a routine play where there was no evidence of malice.

Contact has always been a part of ice hockey, but in this case there wasn't even much contact between the players. Roy, who apparently wanted above all things to play college hockey and who was supported absolutely in that desire by his family, was the victim of bad luck: so bad that it was heart-breaking to witness, and it's impossible to explain.

The great attraction of our games is that they offer the illusion of order in a landscape where there is so often none apparent. So, what happened to Travis Roy is twice ironic. He was doing what he'd trained and practiced to do — what he *loved* to do — and, in doing it, he broke his neck. A broken neck shouldn't ever happen to anyone in any way, but these circumstances are, perhaps, especially poignant. Playing a game governed by rules and the clock, Travis Roy missed a step, and he fell outside the logic of both.

We are a species which craves explanation, and maddeningly — as is so often the case — there is none. Instead, there is the genuine flood of compassion that has come to the Roys from friends and from strangers since the accident. And there is working toward strength and serenity, and hoping that striving toward those qualities will carry Travis Roy and his family into some tolerable place beyond the immediate catastrophe.

Wait 'Til Next Year

Our Christmas tree went up Monday evening, and no casual observer would know there's anything wrong with it . . . But I do.

It's a reasonably ample evergreen . . . a real tree, a little over six feet tall. The little needles are still supple. Almost all the lights work, and I tucked the ones that don't far enough into the branches to that they won't show. The tree's covered with bright balls, puffy Santas, silvery snowflakes, and some handcrafted, red and green pipe-cleaner somethings. Most of the really large ornaments are toward the bottom of the tree; the smallest, most fragile decorations are up high; and a red-capped elf smiles down on everything from the top branch.

But the cheerful red and white ornament featuring the Boston Red Sox logo — tasteful glass it is, nothing plastic about it — has been returned to the attic like some superfluous middle reliever gone to the bullpen.

And the splendid horse and jockey ornament has been put out to pasture there, too. the rider's silks are bright; the horse's ears lie flat against his head. I brought this beauty home from the track at Saratoga a couple of summers ago . . . I know that, because it says "Saratoga" across the bottom, right under the running horse's running legs. Talk about a class Christmas tree ornament.

Last year these decorations would have hung with the Santas and icicles, but this year it's my wife's turn to say which baubles make the cut, and she's ruled the sports stuff out. Ten or twelve years ago, we had a debate over whether there should be tinsel. That's what led to our compromise: one year it's her tree to decorate, the next year it's mine. When our kids got old enough to help with the decorating, we both ruled out tinsel, but the alternating years scheme has remained, and this time around it's Mary's call. Fair is fair. My protest was perfunctory. I put the Red Sox ornament and the horse and rider back in the box with a shrug, and I didn't even tell Mary about the little, leather soccer ball dangling from a Christmas-red string, which a colleague gave me this season. But drop me a line if you know where I can find, say, a tasteful little Gump Worsley goalie figure, or something in a crossed tennis racquets motif . . . maybe a bobble-head football doll for the top of the tree where the elf stands now . . . because it's never too early to begin Christmas preparations.

⚑

CHRISTMAS WISH

I remember a Christmas wish, one I had over 30 years ago. It was actually a year-round wish, but it was particularly vivid at Christmas time, because that's the season everybody associates with wishes which Santa Claus will address.

It was a simple wish. I wished that Willie Mays, who played centerfield magically for the New York Giants in those days, would move in next door to my family. That way, Willie and I could play catch when he came home from the Polo Grounds, or before he left for the ballpark, if he wanted to warm up. And in his spare time in the twilight of weekend evenings — say, when the day games were over, and all up and down the street fathers were getting their grills ready for cookouts — he would work with me on my batting stance and show me how to get a jump on the ball . . . fine tuning my skills so that when the time came, I'd be ready to step into centerfield for the Giants to take his place.

In my six- or seven-year-old head this did not seem a preposterous wish. I grew up less than an hour from the Polo Grounds by car. The house next door to ours, separated only by the width of two driveways, was a perfectly nice house. It was too big for the people living there, an older couple whose children were grown and gone. Everybody said they'd be selling the house to somebody . . . Why not to Willie Mays?

As far as I was concerned, the sooner the better. The older couple had three lean and intimidating boxer dogs. I was sure Willie Mays would have a cheerful mutt like the dog I grew up with, and they could play together in foul territory while Willie patiently taught me all I'd need to know.

We already had the ballfield for it. My father had laid it out in the backyard, striding off the lines and sinking flat stones in the grass for bases. It was a little uneven where left field dipped to begin a slope down to where the apple tree was, but it was a serviceable little park. Over the garage that would be Willie's was a home run.

But, of course, it didn't happen.

And when I was eight years old, Willie's employers — through greed and treachery a child could not possibly understand — moved his team to California. *The World Telegram and Sun*, which my father brought home from work every night, continued for a while to cover the Giants as if they were still the home team, but it wasn't the same. The dream was dead. Even at eight, I knew nobody could commute from northern New Jersey to a ballpark in San Francisco. Come to think of it, the Santa Claus story must have begun to feel pretty unlikely by then, too.

That was all 30 years ago, and since then much has changed. Willie Mays has gray hair, and because of his association with various casinos, he needed a special dispensation from the commissioner's office a while back to return to baseball. The fine man who carefully laid out the diamond in the backyard has died. He left a granddaughter, though, and even if she doesn't know it yet, her time for Santa Claus and Christmas dreams will come. I'll have to be ready soon. I'll have to be prepared. Maybe that's why I've found myself remembering the wish about Willie Mays and the house next door.

⚑

Remembering Hedgehog

"I can't do it!" she shrieks.

My seven-year-old daughter, Alison, is sprawled halfway up a hill, halfway around a cross-country ski loop which some idiot named *The Big Easy*.

She turns her face into the wet snow. Her brand new skis are crossed, her mittens are soaked, she wants to go back.

"Going back would take as long as going forward," I tell her, though I have no idea whether it's true. The map is hopeless. It doesn't show hills like the one on which we're stalled. But I'm the dad, so I have to sound as if I know what I'm doing.

"Get up over the center of your skis, stand up, and I'll help you up the hill."

"I hate this," Alison mutters. No seven-year-old should sound so weary.

Just before Christmas, cross-country skis for the whole family seemed like such a good idea. Now, on this brilliant day for skiing on this golf course in Maine groomed for the sport, Alison would sell her skis for kindling. No, she would pay someone to remove and bury them.

Amy, my older daughter, had mastered the sport in 10 minutes. She is far ahead on the trail, occasionally looking back in derision, thinking up names to call her slipping, sprawling younger sister. Oh, yes, one of the truly great family gift ideas.

Finally on her feet, Alison — with my hand on her back — is making minimal progress: a step forward, a slide back, a flailing pole, another half-step forward. We try pointing her ski tips out. We try side-stepping. Eventually, we make it to the top of the hill.

Alison sighs. "It's big, but it's *not* easy," she says.

I nod in agreement. We plug along.

By now, her mother and her sister are out of sight. Maybe they are already making us lunch. This family adventure has become an adventure that has split our family in half.

Around the next bend we catch sight of the road. "Alison, if we cut over from here, I think we can walk home in just a few minutes."

She nods her tired, wet head. She would rather walk to Chicago that ski another hundred yards.

But on the next morning — gray, misty, unpromising — we luck out. Amy and I go out for a quick glide on a trail called *Hedgehog*. It's easier than *The Big Easy* and not as big. It weaves in and out of the quiet woods, crosses a brook, and looks everywhere like a postcard advertisement for cross-country skiing.

Amy suggests that we go back and get mom and Alison. "She'd love this trail," Amy says. "No hills." My thoughtful daughter . . . my daughter, the altruist.

So, we return and collect Alison and mom. And it works. Everyone loves *Hedgehog*. Alison glides along like a champ. I even remember the camera, and at an especially scenic spot we encounter a solo skier who agrees to take a picture of the four of us: the skiing family, all four members together, smiling.

No one who gets our Christmas card next year need know that it was ever otherwise.

SEASON'S GREETINGS

I wish you all pitches
    As fat and as high
As a big, harvest moon
    In a black background sky
And umpires who figure
    When they make a call
That, if you don't hit it,
    It must be a ball.

May you have your best year
    When your contract runs out
And get signed for 10 million,
    Despite lurking doubt
That you're human and, therefore,
    Not worth more than eight.
Then, may you hit .400
    And know you're that great.

May the basketball feel like
    An egg in your hand.
When you drive may the defense
    Be knee-deep in sand.
May your touch be as fine
    As a new baby's hair.
When you finish each pivot,
    May your knees still be there.

May the surgeons look elsewhere
    To fund all their pensions.
May the newspaper lay
    On you positive mentions.

May each spiral you throw
  Be as straight as a string;
May the guy on the other end
  Catch the damn thing;
And may linemen who rush you
  Like barreling trains
Bang into each other
  And bruise their own brains.

May your serves all catch tape,
  All your shots have their stuff,
And may all your opponents
  Have manners enough
To refrain from embarrassing
  You and the sport
By whining and wailing
  All over the court.

May your putting improve
  Even as your drives fade
So the gal'ry won't notice
  The progress time's made,
And when you slow down or
  Decide to relax,
May a Seniors Tour keep you
  In greens fees and slacks.

May you roll only strikes, or
  At worst, maybe spares,
Your gutter balls witnessed
  By no one who cares.

May you kick from the blocks
  At the sound of the gun
And finish successf'ly each
  Race that you run.

If sailing's your sport, may
  Your winds all be right.
May you keep dry and warm
  And be home ev'ry night.

And if boxing's the only game
  Where you can find

Real excitement, may you
    Soon recover your mind.

May the horses you bet on
    Run better than mine . . .
To say they run *at all*
    Would be more than just kind.

May the college you love
    Keep its sports programs clean,
No player accepting
    So much as a bean,
No graduate screaming,
    "The coach should be canned!"
'Cause the team hasn't done
    Quite as well as he'd planned.

If your town has no cable,
    May it soon see the light
So the games on your tube
    Can be merry and bright,
And when those games fall over
    The edge of the night,
May your spouse understand,
    Or almost, if not quite.

I wish you great seats and
    Hot franks, cold ice cream,
And a home club that's good enough
    So you can dream;
And people to share it,
    Help carry the load
When a prince of a player
    Turns into a toad;
And to share it, as well, when
    The foul ball bends fair
And delirious shouts split
    The ballpark's charged air.

May you star in the clutch.
    May you not miss a sign.
Happy holidays, all, to
    Your home team from mine.

BATS REMEMBERED

I hope somebody gives me a baseball bat this year. It ought to be a wooden one, not one of those everlasting aluminum models that goes *ping* instead of *crack*. All the good bats I ever got were made of wood.

When I was nine, my father said he'd take me anywhere I wanted to go for my birthday, and I told him the Baseball Hall of Fame in Cooperstown, New York. Though it was at least a half day's drive away, he never flinched. I put on my New York Giants uniform and off we went.

When we'd finished touring the Hall about 11 times, my father waited while the salesman in the souvenir shop took one bat after another out of the rack they were hanging from so I could swing each one and make my choice. I picked an Adirondack: white from the knob to halfway up the barrel; light brown from there to the heavy end of the bat. It was an Andre Rodgers Model. Rodgers was a rookie shortstop with the Giants then, and in the following 11 years he hit only .249, but they made a terrific bat under his signature. Some kid on my Little League team broke it eventually, but I put a screw through it and taped it up and kept it around for years.

The only time anyone actually gave me a bat for Christmas was six or seven years ago, when my wife and I were visiting her family in Pennsylvania. Frustrated by my inability to provide her with a Christmas list, Mary drove me into town and then led me to the basement of a wonderful sporting goods store . . . a warehouse of bats.

"Pick any one you want," my wife said. And then she and the salesman watched me heft and swing and run my thumb over many candidates before finding the right bat. My wife says she hates baseball, but she never snickered or rolled her eyes or even looked at her watch. Not once.

Anyway, that one was broken the following summer during a batting practice. The other players on my team, all of whom had long since switched to aluminum bats, cheered derisively. A cruel thing.

The only wooden bat I have now is sort of an ornamental model. Where most bats have a player's name (like my Andre Rodgers bat did), this one says *Cooperstown — The Home of Baseball*, and the label reads, *Cooperstown Bat Company*. I got it the second time I visited the Hall of Fame, two years ago last October. My father was with me that time, too, and once again, the trip was my idea. He remembered the Rodgers Model and said he'd like to buy me another bat, so I went along with it, even though it meant taking a half dozen into the street on that half-dark Cooperstown afternoon, because there wasn't room for practice swings in the store. So that bat's a souvenir of the last trip I took with my father, who was already sick that fall, although neither of us knew it. He was dead a year later.

Recently, a guy who works for a big bat manufacturer down south told me that *his* company makes the bats that say *Cooperstown* on them, a revelation harmonious with the mistaken notions that Abner Doubleday invented baseball and that the first game was played in that sleepy New York town. But the guy didn't touch me with that unhappy, commercial fact: the revelation that a *Cooperstown* bat was in some sense a fraud. Because there was nothing false or hollow about an old man buying his nearly middle-aged son another bat, even if it was two months to Christmas that afternoon. Quite the contrary, I was moved.

And so I hope somebody gives me a baseball bat this year. Because I'd like to take a wooden one with me into the spring, but I won't use the *Cooperstown* bat. I'm not going to submit it to the rigors of curveballs in on the fists during a game, or even in batting practice. I don't want to see that one crack, wherever it was made.

JOHN LUCAS

Though it is only January, I'm ready to submit my nomination for NBA coach of the year.

John Lucas represents a success story unprecedented even in sports, where one team of two succeeds every night. As a player, Lucas was quick, inventive, and consistently self-destructive. His 14-year career as a point guard in the NBA was interrupted by drug and alcohol addiction. His own on-going recovery began in 1986, and shortly thereafter Lucas started spreading the good news. He put together a rehab program for players and ex-players, and his commitment to the project has been as personal as it gets.

Last year, ex-Dallas Maverick player Roy Tarpley was scheduled to leave Lucas' program for a tryout in the Continental Basketball Association. When Tarpley admitted to Lucas that he was afraid to go alone because he wasn't sure enough of his sobriety, Lucas nodded and agreed to go along. As Tarpley's 38-year-old escort, he played one CBA game in Wichita Falls and logged 23 assists.

The previous year, John Lucas had acquired the Miami Tropics of the US Basketball Association in an effort to create for some of his fellow-recovering addicts conditions similar to those the players would face when they tried to resume their careers. Lucas ended up coaching as well as owning the

Tropics because, as he said, all the other candidates he interviewed for the job "were only all about winning."

Lucas himself has learned to be about something more. "My focus isn't all about winning," he recently told a *New York Times* writer. "It's about helping people."

Despite that frankly heretical credo, on December 18th John Lucas was hired to coach the San Antonio Spurs, an underachieving outfit which had stumbled early under the guidance of Jerry Tarkanian. Along with a few stars, such as center David Robinson, Lucas inherited two graduates of his own recovery center: William Bedford and Lloyd Daniels. As the first former addict hired to coach a major sports team, John Lucas appeared to be a man in the right place at the right time, as least if he relished a challenge.

Though San Antonio has been remarkably successful since John Lucas took over as coach, it is too early to pronounce this elevation of helping people over the great god Winning a success. As any ex-addict knows, it will always be too early. If addicts learn anything, they learn to take recovery one day at a time. But it is not too early to applaud Lucas for what he has already accomplished by placing winning, basketball, and money in a context that so often eludes athletes, as well as the rest of us.

However the *X*s and *O*s and *W*s and *L*s shake down from now until June, John Lucas has already reminded the NBA and its fans that wisdom, patience, faith, and helping people are larger matters.

ᕒ

HOLMES VS. TYSON

The sports page was cold as the winter
    With news that's a far cry from new,
An ex-heavyweight is a loser,
    And he doesn't know what he's been through.
Larry Holmes made, they say, some three million,
    Though the fight was lopsided and rank,
But he said to reporters that evening
    That he'd laugh all the way to the bank.
Then he said that he'd party tomorrow,
    Next day, and the day after that,
But I wonder how long you can party
    When the lights go out under your hat?
Some still call the fight game *the sweet science.*
    Maybe music fills Larry Holmes' dreams,
But while those sweet birds sing in his attic,
    There's termites in all of the beams.
What do they think — these fighters, these boxers —
    When they read or they hear all the studies
That prove that the jabs and the hooks and the crosses
    Have rattled the brains of their buddies?
Do they figure it's bleeding-heart sissies
    Or racists who knock the fight game
'Cause it offers poor black kids escape from the ghetto,
    A shot at big money and fame?
My heart bleeds, all right, for the fighters —
    Ray Robinson, Louis, Ali —

212

And unknowns who fade into the shadows,
So much less than what they used to be.
What's the use in escape from the ghetto
If you wind up with scars on your brain
That tie-up your tongue and scramble your thoughts?
Maybe that's why they all fight again.
Larry Holmes says he'll party tomorrow,
Next day, and the day after that,
But I wonder how long you can party
When the lights go out under your hat?

Now Holmes versus Tyson is hist'ry,
No surprises, not much of a fight,
The old guy got knocked down three times in the 4th round
And they tell me that he's got the right
To mortgage his brain for a pay day
And the fun that the crowd came to see.
They also say it's a free country,
And I guess that that means we're all free
To watch as the Moores and the Kims and Parets
Get killed on the cable TV;
To watch as a champ like Muhammad,
Once dazzling and quick, sharp and funny,
Goes slurring and stumbling down Dream Street,
And we say, "Sure, but look at the money."
To watch as the next former champion
Falls slack, dumb, and lost at our feet,
And later says we shouldn't worry
The party starts now. It's his treat.

And the party will go through tomorrow,
Next day, and the day after that.
And we'll watch him and hope he enjoys it
'Til the lights go out under his hat.

PRETEND BASEBALL

For years now, people have been urging me to write something about Rotisserie League Baseball.

"It's great," they say. "You get to draft players like the real owners do. Then the team you put together competes with the teams the other owners in your league put together, according to the statistics the real players generate. You wouldn't believe how people get caught up in it."

I know all this. Several years ago a friend of mine from California visited for a few days. Three or four times a day he phoned the other owners in his Rotisserie League to arrange trades. His mind worked constantly on it. Last spring he called to ask me how many at-bats I thought Carlos Quintana would get. This is the sort of question that occupies Rotisserie League Baseball Team owners.

But I never have written about Rotisserie League Baseball, because it bears about the same relationship to real baseball as voting for players in the All-Star Game bears to playing in it.

I did write once about a dice baseball league. That was because one of the players in it had been divorced by his wife, but she came back to him, and the guys in the league swore it was because — late at night, lying in bed — she missed the oddly comforting, constant rattle of dice on the kitchen table below.

Rotisserie League Baseball offers no such myths. You draft your players, you pay the appropriate fees to the league treasurer, then you wait for the computer firm you have all hired to spit out the statistical analysis by which the teams in your league are ranked, and by which the entry fees are redistributed. You don't even need baseball cards to play Rotisserie League Baseball. In fact, they'd get in the way. You might be persuaded to draft a utility infielder by the glint of confidence in his eye, only to see him finish the season in Pawtucket or Rochester, where even the most flamboyant statistics will do your paper team no good. Best to base your choices strictly on math . . . anathema to me. I took first-year Algebra *three* times and passed at last only because I swore to my beleaguered teacher that I would never tell anyone I'd been in his class.

So I come by my antipathy to Rotisserie League Baseball honestly. But now it is time to burst past that antipathy and champion the rights of those who love it, for their rights are in danger. The Attorney General of the State of Florida has issued an opinion declaring fantasy sports leagues as a form of illegal gambling, though it does not comment on whether they are dumb. The opinion is long and full of citations from the appropriate statutes. It gives every impression that Florida is cranking-up its resources to nail dangerous fantasy league players wherever they may be practicing their game.

And so I say, ease up, Mr. Attorney General of Florida. Concentrate on drug-runners and fly-by-night real estate operators down there. And while you're at it, check the statutes to see if there's anything that limits the number of fast food franchises per acre, because you've got to be over the limit if there is. Turn your guns on something more threatening than fantasy leaguers, no matter how their particular avocation has grown and prospered, or else I shall be forced to call for a national hunkering-down in sympathy and support for the right to be silly at will.

R

WINTERY THOUGHTS

When we are children, we dream of doing wondrous things before throngs of admiring fans while delirious, play-by-play men shout out our names until they are hoarse. Or, at least, some of us do.

When I was little, I played a make-shift, solitary baseball game by throwing a tennis ball against the garage in back of our house. If I hit one of the panels in the door, I got a grounder, which I'd throw against the door again: out at first, routine play. A ball against the roof would come back a fly, which was also a routine play. There was a gutter running along the edge of the roof, though, and if I hit the lip of the gutter just right, the ball would take off, sail out over the iris bed and into the backyard . . . the bleachers. I aimed for that place whenever the Giants were down a run in the bottom of the ninth, Willie Mays was on first, and I was up. And some afternoons I hit a lot of foul balls until I could find the spot on the gutter and win the game with the "longest homerun in the Polo Grounds *anybody* has *ever* seen! *Ahhhh!*"

I could do it as a football player, too . . . throwing passes to myself and making spectacular catches, invariably falling over the goal line, sometimes spitting out imaginary teeth and blood when I got up again. I could do it on the living room carpet if it was raining out.

At one point, my father put up a basketball hoop on a pole in the backyard — a considerable triumph for a man who had thumbs for fingers — and never mind that somebody backed the car into the pole before the cement around it was dry, so that the backboard ever after kicked out even the softest jumper as if it were coming from a slingshot. It was my home court, and on it the clock invariably showed just enough time for me to toss in the game-winner, no matter how many rebounds I had to get to do it.

Later I did it as a hockey player, too . . . firing pucks past a phantom goalie into the pocked beaverboard in the cellar and wrecking the room for anything else.

But somewhere along the line my perspective changed. So when I watched the little bit of the Super Bowl that I watched on Sunday, I found myself thinking about the Denver receivers (who kept dropping passes when it might have mattered whether they caught them or not) and the Denver defensive backs (who kept futilely chasing Jerry Rice when it certainly did not matter at all, because no bookie anywhere ever gave anybody 46 points on anything).

When I see basketball, sometimes, I find myself watching the guy who gets his pocket picked and stands flat-footed and dumbfounded while the man who stole the ball streaks the length of the court and dunks it. The other night the sportscast showed a hockey player inadvertently slipping the puck past his own goaltender, and I didn't laugh, though that seemed to be what the guy who'd picked out the video clip thought I should do. Even baseball's not immune. I study the pitcher who looks back over his shoulder at the homerun that's just settling into the seats 360 feet away, or the infielder who's staring, baffled, at his glove after a ground ball has just kicked under it.

I see these things, and I think to myself, "Well, if I were out there, that could happen to me, too. It's not written anywhere that I have to catch the winning touchdown, or hit the homerun that brings the whole park to its feet, is it? I could be called for traveling, or even fan on a slap shot just as time ran out."

These are wintery thoughts, and it may be that one of the many things that separates me from pro athletes is that I think this way sometimes, and they don't. Or, at least, those I've talked to have told me that they don't. Which — in a funny sort of way — is too bad for them. Because it means they have no occasion to close their eyes as I do sometimes to imagine, in self-defense, I suppose, the gutter on the garage and the rickety backboard and the backyard goal line and the beat-up basement . . . *Homerun! Basket! Touchdown! Score!*

GUTTER BALLS

I had remembered bowling as a very forgiving game in which people don't get hurt and nothing much can go wrong. So, on a recent, wet weekend afternoon, it seemed like a good idea to take the family out to the candlepin lanes.

Once there, things began to go wrong right away. In her very first frame, Alison (my younger daughter, who is five) knocked down two pins. They fell slowly — reluctantly — but they fell. This would have been fine, except that Amy (my older daughter, who is eight) bowled three gutter balls in her first frame and concluded that bowling was stupid.

By the third frame, I was ready to agree with her. That was when the younger daughter threw two balls that never got going fast enough to make it to the end of the gutter. Each rolled for a while and then came gently to a stop, as if it had gotten tired or run out of fuel.

I had never seen this happen before, but I understood pretty much right away that I had two options. I could walk self-consciously down the alley, pick up the balls, and bring them back to the ball rack; or I could wind-up and wing a ball down the gutter just hard enough to knock the inert balls past the pins.

I chose to do the former, though I felt like a fool. With each step I expected to hear the owner of the alleys shout,

"Hey, you blockhead! What are you doing down by those pins?" But he didn't, and nobody laughed.

When it was Alison's turn to bowl again, I told her to try to roll the ball a little harder. For a frame or two, she did. And though she didn't knock down any pins, all the balls made it to the end of the alley. This seemed to please her, and it certainly pleased me.

Meanwhile, my wife — who was scoring considerably better than both of the kids, but had fallen behind me — began to needle.

"You're so competitive," she said. "Every time you throw the ball, you get this look on your face like you want to break the pins into kindling."

"I'm just trying to knock them down," I told her. "That's the point."

"The point is to have fun," she said. "Don't look so grim about it."

Maybe I was looking grim because of a premonition of what would happen next.

Returning from her seventh or eighth trip to the drinking fountain, Alison nudged a couple more balls about three-quarters of the way down the right hand gutter, where they quietly came to rest. This time I decided to knock them the rest of the way home.

I wound up — probably looking *very* grim — and fired a ball directly down the gutter. It was, unfortunately, careening side-to-side within the gutter when it hit the closer stalled ball and — although both of Alison's balls rolled obediently into the pit behind the pins — my shot bounced completely over our alley and crashed into the pins on the adjacent lane. That probably surprised the man who was bowling there, although I am not sure of that, because I couldn't meet his eyes.

"Do those pins count on your score?" Amy shouted.

"Absolutely!" I said.

"No fair," she said, and my wife told me again that I shouldn't throw the ball so hard.

By the time we'd reached the final frames, Alison was slithering like a snake around the molded plastic seat, and Amy had begun walking away from each shot without waiting to see where the ball went. But, weirdly, when the game was over, they both wanted to bowl another string.

"No," I told them. "It's time to go. Maybe we'll come back another day."

And maybe, if I can ever forget almost everything that happened that day, we will.

DURING DESERT WAR

A sports writer traveling through the South recently reported that when the athletic departments at a few of the major basketball schools were slow to sew American flag patches on the uniforms of their players, the crowds and the editorial writers let them have it. All the players down there are wearing flag patches now.

Seton Hall University made the patches available to their basketball players earlier this season. One player, an Italian named Marco Locar, chose not to wear the patch. His coach supported the decision, but many of the people who came to watch the team play did not. When Seton Hall met St. John's in Madison Square Garden two weeks ago, many of those present jeered Locar each time he touched the ball.

He began to receive hate mail, which upset his pregnant wife enough so that eventually Locar left the team and the University, and returned with his wife to Italy. Before he left, he expressed surprise that people could not accept his belief that wearing the flag would have constituted support for war, which would have been against his beliefs as a Christian.

This sort of story is not limited to the world of sports. In a suburban Boston neighborhood close to where I live, a friend of mine recently got a letter addressed to himself, his wife, and his two children. In essence, the letter said,

"Everybody else on the street is flying the American flag. Where's yours?"

If war brings out the best in some — extraordinary acts of sacrifice and selflessness — it also brings out the worst. A crowd at a sporting event, like a crowd anywhere, is particularly susceptible to the sort of stupid and cruel hysteria that hounded Marco Locar from this country.

When an arena full of people shouts *USA! USA!*, the line between healthy pride and vicious, mindless jingoism is always hard to identify. And the shift toward the vicious and the mindless is becoming more pronounced as the war goes on, with the mindless perhaps pulling into the lead.

Maybe it's because President Bush made such a point of coupling our games with the war by appearing on TV at half-time during the Super Bowl and for a few minutes before the NBA All-Star Game.

Maybe it's just because making money never stops being important in this country, war or no war. For whatever reason, the Topps Bubble Gum Company — previously known for marketing baseball cards — is now offering us a line of war cards, pictures of generals and tanks and fighter planes. I hesitate to think what the statistics on the back will document.

Patriotism is a funny business, isn't it? The cameras at the All-Star Game showed several women wearing sweaters and earrings featuring the American flag. Twenty years ago, wearing a shirt with an American flag design was a good way to get arrested in some states.

These days, those of us who do not choose to wear our patriotism on our sleeves, or in our ear lobes, or to fly it from a flag pole where we live, run a risk. If you believe that war is worse than pointless — certain to kill thousands of people, combatants and civilians alike — and that the flag has become the symbol of people who endorse the killing; if you are convinced that the best way to support the troops is to work to end the war, so that they will return home alive and whole, and that the commitment to achieving peace without recourse to bombing would finally be more courageous than making war, you might want to stay out of crowded basketball arenas or hockey rinks for now.

May the sun soon shine again on those of us who are not wearing the flag.

May we all be luckier than Marco Locar.

No Game Today

Some of the games have already been postoned, and perhaps others should have been. Witnesses at Boston Garden Wednesday night say there were those who felt sheepish for being there, and lots of the people who'd paid to see the Celtics kept leaving their seats to check Dan Rather or Peter Jennings on one of the TV sets in the lobby.

It is a dumb cliché to suggest that the big game of war dwarfs all the little games we would otherwise take so seriously, but it's a dumb cliché with some impact at this point. The fact is that sports and the way we understand them have affected the way we process what's coming at us from the war now. One of the first pilots interviewed after the fighter planes had begun returning from Baghdad said, "It was like being a pro athlete heading into his first game, but then the other team didn't show up."

Sports provided the metaphor with which this young man could explain the experience of dropping bombs from an airplane. It seemed harmless enough and natural. Certainly war has been providing our games with metaphors for as long as we can remember.

But finally the language of sports is the wrong language for war. We will mix them up now. We will ask ourselves and each other how the troops are doing, and we'll compare real

225

body counts with the estimates. We'll be tempted, no matter what our politics, to oversimplify — in a manner that would be appropriate to sports — the complicated circumstances and motivations of the men and women who are at the grim work in the Middle East, as well as that of the men and women and boys and girls who are protesting the doing of that grim work. We will assume — for the sake of simplicity and our own stability — that people who live in different nations can be temporarily labeled *good guys* or *bad guys* as easily as the ballplayers in different uniforms.

By the constant coverage and the precise details about fire power and the maps full of arrows like so many *X*s and *O*s, we'll be tempted to respond to the war as we respond to our games. We'll be tempted to forget that while the latter represent some of our most intricate and enduring entertainments, the former only embodies the shame and sadness we should feel as a species for not having discovered another way.

⚑

SHOES

I guess I've been a little slow to appreciate the seriousness of gym shoes. That's not to say that I haven't known for years that you don't buy the same sneakers to run in that you would buy to walk in. I learned that quite a while back when I asked for a comfortable pair of sneakers over at the mall one day, and when I'd finished paying for them, the woman who sold them to me shook her finger and said, "I better not find out that you've been *running* in these."

"No chance," I told her defensively. "Nothing more than an occasional, half-hearted lope, I swear." I didn't think it was funny.

I've seen the TV ads this winter for the basketball shoes you pump up, though I admit that the first time I learned of them I — like the bemused NBA star who was giggling about them — thought the manufacturer was putting me on.

But I know now that it is no joke. The *Sports Illustrated* in front of me has an eight-page ad for gym shoes (the word *sneaker* appears nowhere) . . . and it is a very beautiful ad, too. There are 20 different models of shoes, and colors like green, yellow, pink, blue and salmon predominate in the trim although on one page the more spectaclar models are bracketed by a very small white shoe and a very small black shoe, as if to demonstrate that even if you have no imagination, this company will condescend to deal with you.

And it does not stop with the colors. The copy claims that these shoes are not only "like nothing you've ever seen before," they "have tongues you can squeeze," they "return your energy," and they "defy gravity." This last may be something basketball leagues have to investigate. You can't legally cork a baseball bat, and it seems to me there are regulations restricting the material you can use to make a pole vaulting pole. Is it fair if one player is wearing shoes which defy gravity and the guy who's guarding him isn't?

Some models "move beneath your feet," which sounds a little spooky. And there's one that — again, I'm quoting here — "defies you to stand still." If the money's right, I'm willing to accept that challenge. I've yet to meet the pair of shoes I can't stand still in, even if the band's *really* hot.

Back in the 70s sometime, Tom McGuane wrote a terrific movie called *Rancho Deluxe*, in which an old, beat-up Indian explained to his son why none of them would ever get ahead.

"It's the damn pick-up trucks," he said. "Every time anybody around here gets two or three hundred dollars up, he goes down to the dealer and trades in his pick-up truck for a new one."

I wonder if in the 90s it'll be like that with the playground kids and gym shoes? They are as sleek and alluring as trucks, these pink and purple, gravity-defying energy systems for your feet . . . almost too pretty to wear out into the messy world.

And though there's no mention of price in the eight-page ad, I've done some investigating, and it turns out the top-of-the-line gym shoe in this collection goes for $175 . . . which is how I know that this is a *very* serious subject after all.

ط

THE CENTER OF TWO WORLDS

What initially drew *Sports Illustrated*'s Leigh Montville to Manute Bol was hyperbole. Bol is 7'6" tall, but that is only the beginning. He came from the Sudan and entered this country without a cent in his pocket or a word of English at his command. Then Cleveland State University basketball coach Kevin Mackey tried to get his college to enroll Manute, though Manute had never attended any school anywhere for even a day. He couldn't read or write in any language. Telephones and Coke machines were among the mysteries he had not previously encountered.

Everywhere Manute Bol has played basketball — for the University of Bridgeport, for the Rhode Island Gulls, and for several NBA teams — he has blown people's minds. On his best days, he has bent the game itself into a new shape. In the NBA, he has blocked the shots of some of the world's greatest shooters, and then smiled at them and said, "Don't you watch television? Don't you know you can't do that?"

But basketball itself is only the beginning. Manute has traveled back to the Sudan to visit the refugee camps. There he has seen his former neighbors, his friends, the best man at his wedding. He did what he could to help. He paid for housing and food for many people and worked with Oxfam America to publicize the terrible need. Then he has returned to the U.S. to play basketball for more than a million dollars per year, though on the pro level he has never really been much more than a unique, short-term, one-man defensive strategy. One columnist went so far as to call him the *worst* player in the league . . . which is just another line of hyperbole.

After I read Montville's book, I found myself telling a lot of people about it. One friend — an especially thoughtful man — listened to my account of this 7'6" millionaire walking among his naked, starving brothers and sisters.

"He is all the contradictions of the human condition wrapped in one skin, isn't he?" my friend said.

He was right. Manute has made the longs journeys — from the desert to the city, from poor to rich — and he has left nothing behind. As he departed the refugee camp, companions heard Manute mutter, "I'm dead . . . I'm dead."

Maybe that is what drew Leigh Montville to take on the project of this book. Happily, Montville is writer enough to handle the giant and his journey with wit, grace, and courage. He does not flinch at what is gruesome, and he recognizes the fun in the triumph of Manute's adjustment to the niche he's made for himself in this wired and sports-obsessed country far from the home to which he can no longer return, because he has expressed his outrage at the interference of politics with feeding the people.

You'll find *Manute: The Center of Two Worlds* with the other books about games and athletes, but that's arbitrary. It could be with the sociology books, or those about politics, or even among the theology texts. Toward the end of this book, Montville writes of having heard Manute say, "Who knows what God is dreaming for us?"

Good question.

Good book.

ɮ

FOR COUNTRY

A few months ago, Larry Bird, the multi-millionaire forward for the Boston Celtics, was asked by a reporter whether he'd like to represent the United States in the Olympics in 1992. Bird said he thought not, because by participating he'd perhaps be depriving some deserving college hoopster from the opportunity to play. It sounded like an honest and straightforward answer, so — of course — it didn't hold up. Bird's agent said recently that his guy might be changing his mind.

To be fair to Bird and his agent, circumstances had changed. Panic over the fact that US teams have been losing baseball and basketball tournaments on the international stage convinced the poobahs to eschew sentiment in '92 and send in nothing but pros. By going to Barcelona, Bird might be depriving teammate Kevin McHale of the Olympic thrill, but college boys apparently would not enter into the equation.

And then there is the matter of patriotism. In these days of victory parades and yellow ribbons, you don't lightly reject the opportunity to serve your country, even if the service involved is throwing a ball through a basket for the greater glory of the US Olympic Committee. Ask Michael Jordan.

For remarking that he might prefer to play golf and spend time with his family next summer, he's been slandered as selfish and lacking in concern for the US of A, which — the alleged reasoning goes — will somehow be diminished if it doesn't win a gold medal in basketball next year. There has even been speculation — facetious, I hope — that Jordan's sneaker contract might be jeopardized if the public begins to perceive him as the last communist on earth.

In the hysteria for world basketball domination, we could perhaps use a lesson from recent history. In 1968, Kareem Abdul Jabbar, then a college basketball player known as Lou Alcindor, was urged to leave his summer job working with disadvantaged children in Harlem to lead the US basketball team to a gold medal in Mexico. After some consideration, the thoughtful young giant decided that what he was doing for the kids in New York was more important than what he might do in the Olympics. He stayed on the playgrounds. That was a decision born of conscience, and an act of genuine patriotism.

ß

Bird

There was a statue of him even before he retired.

Larry Bird, still an active Celtic, posed for it several times in the Rhode Island studio of sculptor Armond Lamontagne, who remembers several of their conversations vividly.

"From one window of the studio, you can look over a stone wall to a corn field," Lamontagne told me several years ago. "One day Larry looked out that window at the corn, which was maybe 100 feet away, and he asked me whose it was. I told him there was a farmer who rented the land and came by to work it.

"Larry said, 'Well, you tell him the next time you see him that he's let that corn go too long. It's not gonna be as sweet as it should be.'

"A couple of days later I saw the farmer out there in the field, and I told him what Larry had said. The farmer told me that his wife had been sick and taking care of her had prevented him from picking the corn when he should have done it.

"So Larry was right. And he was right from about 100 feet away."

Part of the hold which Larry Bird has had on Celtics fans in particular and basketball fans in general stems directly from the stubborn residue of the Indiana boy within the basketball millionaire with the aching back. Lunch-pail-types can still identify with Bird's values.

In Monte Carlo last summer — where the Dream Team was preparing to sail through the Olympics — Bird wouldn't buy a beer, because he couldn't believe the price. Never mind that he could have bought the brewery.

Of course, the eye for ripening corn and the frugality wouldn't have gone far toward making Larry Bird a candidate for immortalization if he hadn't also become a superb basketball player: a fellow who worked extraordinarily hard to develop his gifts and to sharpen his skills, thereby becoming not only a champion, but also a player who improved the performance of virtually every teammate he ever had.

Larry Bird was not the tallest or the fastest forward, but he was a superb rebounder, because he was clever and tenacious. He was not the smoothest shooter, but he was an inventive scorer who could find a dozen ways to beat faster, more fluid players. And — as champions must — he played despite damage to his fingers, his back, and the rest of his body that would keep most of us home from easier work.

If, despite all that, it seems silly to you that there is a life-size wooden statue of Larry Bird, and silver coins commemorating his night, and songs to honor him, and so on, consider that there's also an Elvis stamp. Actors get their footprints saved for making us laugh or cry. Presidents — even the really bad ones, even the ones who are crooks — get libraries named after them.

At worst, it's harmless that we should celebrate the career of a fellow whose contribution was hoop savvy and hard labor rather than poetry or military triumph.

And at best, Larry Bird night reminds us to appreciate the wonderful, temporary, and doomed pursuit of excellence, whatever its manifestation.

ᐳ

LIFE ON THE RIM

Over the 1987-88 basketball season, the Albany Patroons
played .889 ball. They lost only one game at home. They won
the championship of the Continental Basketball Association,
and the day after the last game of the playoffs they had no
general manager, no coach, and only one player lined up for
the following season.

That's pretty much the way things go in the CBA, pro
basketball's farm system. Albany's '88-89 season — which
David Levine chronicles in Life on the Rim — was not as
successful, but when you've finished this book, you're likely
to find yourself cheering the Patroons just for making it
through the winter. As the cover suggests, sometimes it was
lonely work. Three players are pictured on folding chairs at
courtside. Behind them stretch endless rows of empty seats.

There is no money in the CBA, where everybody who
lasts makes about $8,000 a season. And almost nobody lasts.
Rosters change at the whim of NBA teams, which are forever
calling up the CBA's best players for 10 days at a time to fill
in for their injured betters, who are — in most cases — not so
very much better. As Levine points out, 90 percent of the
players in the CBA are drafted by NBA teams, many of them
in the first three rounds. Then they don't make it, and oh,
what a falling-off is there.

But those are only facts, and the truth and beauty of *Life on the Rim* is in the anecdotes. Here is some bench chatter from a game between the Patroons and the Wichita Falls Texans. George is George Karl, the Albany coach; Gerald is his General Manager and Assistant Coach.

"Gerald, how many time outs do we have left," barks Karl, his concentration deep into the game . . . Gerald lumbers to the scorer, then lumbers back to report: "Coach, we have two. But they're not too smart here: I think we can get three."

Next stop, Rockford, Illinois for a game against the Lightning, which may or may not be the team which has a water boy who also plays the *Star Spangled Banner* on trumpet each night. Anyway, it's Christmas and the opportunities for celebration or even sustenance in Rockford are limited. Levine's post-game diary entry reads:

"12:45 — We find only another Stop 'n' Go. No beer. No hot food. Buy Christmas dinner: large bag of Doritos, one jar of salsa, one stick of beef jerky, two cans of Spam, one Dolly Madison apple pie, two cherry 7-Ups."

The CBA is a league of vans with flat tires in the desert and of players who may not show up at the next stop and of coaches who should know better . . . pro basketball as Dali might have painted it.

To David Levine's credit, he has not only nailed the absurdity and the attendant humor of this circuit, but also the sadness, even the desperation of young men trying to take themselves seriously as athletes in a league that seems to foil them at every turn. *Life on the Rim* should be required reading for every college basketball hotshot who isn't absolutely certain that he'll make the show, because the message here is, "This could happen to you, big fella . . . Better check into class once in a while so when the coin doesn't drop, you can get yourself a day job."

℞

FOOTBALL HAIKU

Non-believers dismiss the Super Bowl as a bloated celebration of excessive violence and gambling. There is another side to the 29th contest for football supremacy and a trip to Disney World for the winning quarterback.

Here I offer the game's poetic side. I've chosen haiku as the most appropriate form in which to celebrate the Super Bowl phenomenon. The perfect little three-line, 17-syllable poems, like pro football's best moments, are characterized by balance, discipline, and the fragile illusion of meaning in the midst of noisy chaos.

Consider for example, the following haiku from one of the most celebrated of the haiku poets, Issa.

> Look out, my sparrow!
> Fly away! Fly away! See?
> A pony trots by.

Now consider how naturally football assumes the place of Nature for a poet comfortable with this form.

> Look out, you dummy!
> Run away! Run away! *Ahhhhh!*
> Crushed to dust again.

I hope that the following Super Bowl haiku will encourage you to view the game with a serene smile, while others shout, slap the backs of those around them, or — addled with Cheese Doodles, pretzels, and beer — slump, insensible, into the cushions of their sofas.

Long kick, sailing, oh
Catch it? Me? No thank you, no.
I don't wish to die.

Silly coach . . . screaming
You change nothing; the call stands —
But your heart explodes.

Thump! The ball soars, watched.
Three or four billion Chinese,
Bicycling, don't care.

Black bird, black on blue,
Dips above the quarterback,
Unconscious, twitching.

Tired linemen fall
Like candlepins . . . I guess I
Should have gone bowling.

Fingers hunt the ball . . .
The grass blades reach, too; a breeze
Giggles, pushes it.

Game time! Huge lineman,
Frantic, paws through socks, spent tape . . .
Nike swoosh is gone!

Inside the helmet,
Breath echoes, rasps, and echoes.
Cloud is not impressed.

In the big crowd none
Aches, stings, cracks, tears, breaks, or bleeds.
They pay to watch it.

The old quarterback
Stoops, cries, "Three! Red!" Facing him,
Big engines snort, stir.

The fickle crowd's rage
Drifts up, up. Fat owner plots:
New coach? New City?

Decked twice, ears ringing,
Tight end nods, "Okay;" thinks, *Man,
Throw to someone else.*

Clock ticks down to zip.
Twelve-pack is dead and cheese balls
All gone. Nuts all gone.

Winner plays along,
Says, "Me for Disneyland." Thinks:
A beer and a bath.

Grasshopper hops, ducks,
Wide men roar, groan, fall to earth.
Grasshopper ducks, hops.

Garage, dark, empty . . .
Damn! Where is my Bonneville?
Lost on the Chargers.

A star, curious,
Lights the torn tape left behind
For the hungry rat.

From the door, she says,
"Dumb game." He shrugs; says, "Gets worse.
Coming up . . . Bud Bowl."

The gap is here, now:
The back sees it, steps once, and
All the world falls in.

ß

Choosing the Game

One day in the middle of last winter, a baseball fan employed by one of the wire services — finding himself with nothing else to do — compiled a list of major league players who would be paid more than a million dollars for their 1992 summer jobs. I was delighted by the *bulk* of the list on heavy computer paper, each sheet of which was separated by perforations. I took it along to a speaking engagement. I carried it happily to the podium. I told the audience what it was, then held page one of the list up over my head and let the rest of it drop. I'm 6'2" tall, and I have long arms. I couldn't hold the list up high enough for the whole document to fall free, and the last half-dozen pages landed at my feet with a satisfactory *plop!*

People in the audience responded in a variety of ways to my visual aid. Some jumped at the opportunity to rail against baseball players and other athletes as spoiled jerks. Several pointed out that ballplayers were entertainers, and that — as such — the best of them were at least as much entitled to millions of dollars as Clint Eastwood and Sly Stallone — who only *pretend* to accomplish remarkable physical feats — and Johnny Carson — who doesn't really do anything much at all. And, of course, some scholar pointed out that *any* emotional response to the salaries of baseball players was hopelessly foolish, as each player was making precisely what the market had determined he was worth . . . the charmed career of Matt Young notwithstanding.

I have a pretty fair tolerance for discussions like the one summarized above. Often enough to keep them from becoming tedious, somebody tosses a knuckleball into the debate. Once a thoughtful, if quirky, writer told me that he didn't think baseball players were paid *enough*. "They bear our dreams," he said. "Who can put a price on that?"

Finally, of course, and again and again each spring, we have the invitation to visit baseball to see if its economics has spoiled the fun.

So far, the grass still looks green to me. The home uniforms are as white as they were when the futures of the men wearing them were much less secure. When the ledger sheet dictates the razing of Fenway Park, perhaps the intrusion of money's logic on the dreamscape will be inescapable and terminally sad, but for now the ballplayers still look to me like ballplayers, and a day at the park is sweet fun. If my time to cling to that belief (which is foolish, perhaps, but — thank God — stubborn) is short, then more power to tenacity. There are so few venues in which we can afford to ignore the money entirely.

When I began this piece, I looked through my files for the computer printout that listed baseball's wealthiest players. Apparently, I've lost it.

It must be time for Opening Day.

ß

AFTERWORD

A while back at a New Hampshire Humanities Foundation Symposium entitled *Sport and the American Experience*, I found myself in the company of a number of women who are — or have been — extraordinary athletes. From their personal experiences they came up with various perspectives on the status of women in sports today.

Jane Blalock, the winner of 29 tournaments on the LPGA tour through 1985, is a businesswoman now. She told a story of a business appointment she'd had recently at a country club where she is a member. Part way through lunch, a club functionary came to the table and told her she'd have to leave, since women — even businesswomen — weren't allowed in the grille room at that hour.

"I'm sorry," the functionary said.

"Not as sorry as you're *gonna* be," Ms. Blalock told him.

I'm inclined to believe her.

There were other stories about bad old days more distant. One woman in her 50s remembered that during her years as a high school athlete there were no showers in the girls' locker room.

"I guess the idea was that we weren't supposed to sweat," the woman, still an expert skier, shrugged. "And, God help us, we didn't complain."

A third woman, Lee Delfosse, was a member of the US Ski Team 30 years ago and wins Seniors Tennis Tournaments today, so her athletic triumphs have spanned both eras: the one in which the girls had no showers, and the one in which women can't use the grille room for business lunches.

But in talking about sports to a room full of people, Ms. Delfosse was not only upbeat, she was poetic: "I love the excellence which sports has demanded of me," she said. "I can recreate myself each time I compete."

I'm glad she said that. I wish I'd thought of it myself. It makes me feel as if — regarding the issue of the access which girls and women have to the benefits of sports — we haven't entirely failed, though there is considerable distance to go.

A final story from the Humanities Foundation Symposium goes beyond the matter of gender and illuminates the inclination of our culture — and perhaps our species — to twist the positive potential of an athletic achievement into shame and self-loathing.

The storyteller was Penny Pitou. Today, Ms. Pitou is an entrepreneur. She coordinates and escorts ski trips to Europe and hiking expeditions in the Alps. But 35 years ago in Squaw Valley, she became the first American skier to win an Olympic medal in a downhill event. It was a silver medal, and therein hangs a tale. On the very day she won it, she received a visit from the Vice President of the United States.

"I was really thrilled," Penny Pitou recalls. "I was in the dormitory, and somebody came running up the hall to tell me that Richard Nixon was in the lobby, asking for me. He shook my hand, and I can remember seeing the little, black hairs on his nose twitching, and he said, 'Miss Pitou, I understand you came in second. I'm sorry.'

"I told him, 'But, Mr. Vice President, I won a silver medal.'

"He said, 'Yes, but don't feel badly. Tomorrow, you'll have another opportunity to win a gold medal.'

"I was really depressed for about 10 seconds. Then I

realized that, of course, I should be proud of myself for winning the silver medal. In my other event, I won another silver medal, which was great, and I couldn't help giggling about Vice President Nixon probably brooding over the fact that — as far as he was concerned — I'd failed again."

The happy ending to Penny Pitou's story, then and now, is that she could and can see — and thereby help us see — through the assumption, equally stern and silly, that unless you finish first, you're a loser. (Sometimes, in fact, those who finish first are the most spectacular losers, but that's probably fodder for another day's commentary.)

The point here — and it was a point that kept surfacing in the context of the discussion of various sports throughout the symposium — is that, properly understood, our games give our children and the rest of us marvelous opportunities. We can learn and re-learn that working hard at something tends to make us better at it, as well as increase our self-respect. Within the comfortable context of rules, we can know the joy of pushing ourselves, and of growing in strength and grace, and perhaps of accomplishing *more* than we thought we could accomplish.

And if we can only keep our heads on straight when somebody tells us that if we don't finish first, we should be unhappy, much more often than not we'll be better off for having played the game.

៨

ACKNOWLEDGMENTS

My thanks to all the people at *Only A Game* and elsewhere who've helped with suggestions, encouragement, and editing over the years, among them: Gary Waleik, Katy Clark, David Greene, Doug Haslam, Marvin Mandell, Sandy Kaye, Sue Sheppard, Mark Schramm, Tom Goldman, Tony Brooks, John Ogulnik, Hugh Muñoz, Dean Capello, Jennifer Loeb, Karen Given, Jon Marston, and James "George Carter" Isaacs.

Thanks, also, to WBUR folks, past and present, including Iris Adler, Carol Rissman, Pat Bodnar, Lisa Mullins, Jane Cristo, Steve Elman, Sam Fleming, Bruce Gellerman, Olivia Rowan, Rebecca Smuckler, Ken Bader, and a host of others.

To Henry Horenstein, my special thanks for being a good friend and wonderful photographer.

Many thanks to all the people who've written, called, or e-mailed with corrections or encouragement in response to commentaries, books, articles, or *Only A Game*.

And finally, thanks to Don Davidson at The Peninsula Press, who thought that it would be a good idea to compile and publish this collection. His colleagues — Andy Scherding, Casey Waters, Jim Goodnough, and Roxy Hambleton — have all done a fine job of guiding this project along, from the beginning to this very end.